A Guided Reader for Secondary English

A Guided Reader for Secondary English: Pedagogy and Practice draws on extracts from the published work of some of the most influential education writers to provide insight, guidance and clarity about key issues affecting secondary English teachers.

The book brings together key extracts from classic and contemporary writing and contextualizes these in both theoretical and practical terms. The extracts are accompanied by a summary of the key ideas and issues raised, questions to promote discussion and reflective practice, and annotated further reading lists to extend thinking.

Taking a thematic approach and including a short introduction to each theme, the chapters cover:

- Theoretical models of curricular English
- The nature and structure of the secondary school English curriculum
- Historical perspectives
- Texts and intertextuality
- The arts context for secondary English
- Assessment and evaluation
- Linguistic and cultural contexts
- Future possibilities and tensions

D0124815

Aimed at trainee and newly qualified teachers including those working towards Masters-level qualifications, as well as existing teachers, this accessible, but critically provocative, text will be an essential resource for those that wish to deepen their understanding of secondary English education.

David Stevens is Course Director of the PGCE (secondary) course and Subject Tutor for secondary English at the University of Durham, UK.

A Guided Reader for Secondary English

Pedagogy and practice

Edited by
David Stevens

Routledge
Taylor & Francis Group

LONDON AND NEW YORK

First published 2012
by Routledge
2 Park Square, Milton Park, Abingdon, Oxon OX14 4RN

Simultaneously published in the USA and Canada
by Routledge
711 Third Avenue, New York, NY 10017

Routledge is an imprint of the Taylor & Francis Group, an informa business

British Library Cataloguing in Publication Data
A catalogue record for this book is available from the British Library

Library of Congress Cataloging in Publication Data
A guided reader for secondary English: pedagogy and pratice/ [edited by] David Stevens.
 pages cm
Includes bibliographical references.
1. English language—Study and teaching (Secondary)   2. Literature—Study and teaching
(Secondary)   I. Stevens, David, 1947-
LB1631.G785 2012
808'.0420712—dc23

2011051900

ISBN: 978-0-415-61324-8 (hbk)
ISBN: 978-0-415-61325-5 (pbk)
ISBN: 978-0-203-11765-1 (ebk)

Typeset in Bembo
by RefineCatch Limited, Bungay, Suffolk

MIX
Paper from
responsible sources
FSC
www.fsc.org   FSC® C004839

Printed and bound in Great Britain by the MPG Books Group

Contents

Foreword

Various sorts of publication have been available to support the development of professional knowledge amongst secondary teachers. There are some excellent course books, which provide an introduction to teaching generally. These typically assemble chapters on the many areas of work that combine to form contemporary teaching, setting out the wider school and educational context. Then there are volumes specific to a teaching subject, in which practitioners survey various aspects and present accounts of current directions. What David Stevens has put together here differs from either of these undertakings. He has had the notion of a guided reader, which will introduce the central intellectual and theoretical enquiries that have shaped the teaching of English in schools. The outcome is this collection of skilfully chosen excerpts from key writings, organized in thematic chapters, supported and developed by a commentary which outlines questions to be pursued and makes suggestions for further reading.

A principal objective of this project, which will strike a chord with teachers and with teacher educators, has been to find a serviceable method for orienting readers towards the big ideas that have been advanced in English teaching, ideas at a different level from immediate curriculum concerns and teaching decisions. It is safe to say that current teaching has not wanted for support in the immediate tasks of lesson planning and managing classrooms, those absolutely central and important arts. But a serious intention for teachers to develop knowledge of their subject which is 'deep and extensive', in the wording of the presently proposed DfE consultation over standards for 'master teachers',[1] will also value teachers who want rationales for pedagogic choices, who have the ability to stand their ground, theoretically and intellectually, to argue and to innovate and to develop significant work. This requires in turn engagement with ideas and intellectual traditions and, often enough, with sharp debate. To sponsor teachers in developing this level of pedagogic work is one of the important aims of Dr Stevens's collection.

Readers will find a framework that is illuminating but which also offers sufficient breadth and openness to weigh alternatives and make connections. The chapters range from the opening consideration of models for teaching English, through curriculum issues, historical perspectives, teaching texts, English seen from the viewpoint of the arts, assessment, language issues and a look, in closing, towards the future. Each chapter juxtaposes texts and writers, presenting different angles of vision in a manner intended to present several facets of the topic for reflection and for further exploration. For example, in studying the texts that have been gathered round the opening chapter's 'models of English' readers are invited first to juxtapose different versions of critical literacy, then to consider more fully the work of the contemporary scholar of multi-modality and social semiotics Gunther Kress. Having attended also to one critique made of Kress's work, they conclude by balancing John Dixon on 'growth' through English with Peter Griffiths on the implications for approaches to be drawn from literary theory. As will be apparent, there are different questions to ask, in responding to such a selection. What might such writings be said to have in common, which might inform the notion of an English model? Alternatively, what insight can be gained from reflecting on distinctions to be made about the different emphases and rationales evident in these positions? The commentary offers pointers towards such further exploration. There is rich scope for the individual reader, but one can also imagine chapters in this book being taken up by groups, perhaps in teacher INSET sessions, or on training courses, or in study groups, in a spirit of collaborative enquiry.

Not so very long ago, in departments and colleges of education, curriculum subjects, such as English, were thought of principally as a site for passing on teaching methods, in contrast to the grander disciplines of education which formulated foundational theory and undertook research. For English, much attention had been paid to literature, in arguments mainly descending from

1 Proposed Master Teacher Standards, 21 October 2011 (draft): http://media.education. gov.uk/assets/files/pdf/m/draft%20master%20teacher%20standards.pdf

the university, accompanied by some lively writing about school English teaching, centred on the grammar schools since these had been the dominant inheritance. But the aim to develop an intellectual basis for secondary English teaching in this country was something made and constructed, and in some sense fought for, by teachers who pioneered secondary education for all in the years following the Second World War. It was an enterprise that issued also in the formation of subject teaching associations and in the developmental work of some local authorities, supported by an expanding teacher education.

David Stevens's reader is a work in this tradition. The texts that he presents have been researched for a current audience, but have clearly been in part assembled from writings that have had a personal value for him. He draws on wide experience as a teacher, as a teacher educator and researcher, and as a prominent member of the National Association for the Teaching of English. I believe that readers will both enjoy the guidance offered and respond to the commitment to develop work in English at the heart of this important project.

Tony Burgess

Acknowledgements

We are grateful to all those who have granted us permission to reproduce the extracts listed below. While every effort has been made to trace and acknowledge ownership of copyright material used in this volume, the Publishers will be glad to make suitable arrangements with any copyright holders whom it has not been possible to contact.

Morgan, W. (1997) *Critical Literacy in the Classroom*. London: Routledge.

Peim, N. (2009) Transformations: English, Theory and Bernstein, *Changing English* 16.2, 149–164.

Rosen, H. (1977) Out There, or Where the Masons Went, in M. Hoyles (ed.) *The Politics of Literacy*. London: Writers and Readers Publishing Cooperative.

Kress, G. (1995) *Writing the Future: English and the Making of a Culture of Innovation*. Sheffield: NATE.

McGuinn, N. (2005) A Place for the Personal Voice? Gunther Kress and the English Curriculum, *Changing English* 12.2, 205–217.

Dixon, J. (1969) *Growth through English*, Ch. 1 A Method of Definition. Oxford: Oxford University Press.

Griffith, P. (1987) *Literary Theory and English Teaching*. Milton Keynes: Open University Press.

Cox, B. (1995) *Cox on the Battle for the English Curriculum*. London: Hodder & Stoughton.

Scholes, R. (1998) *The Rise and Fall of English*. New Haven, CT: Yale University Press.

West, D. (2008) Changing English, *Changing English* 15.2, 137–143.

Stevens, D. (2011) *Cross-curricular Teaching and Learning in the Secondary School: English*. London: Routledge.

Thomson, J. (2004) New Models of English Teaching, in W. Sawyer and E. Gold (eds) *Reviewing English in the 21st Century*. Melbourne: Phoenix.

Yandell, J. (2008) Mind the Gap: Test and Classroom Literacies, *English in Education* 42.1, 70–87.

Eagleton, T. (1983) *Literary Theory: An Introduction*, Ch. 1 The Rise of English. London: Blackwell.

Knight, R. (1996) *Valuing English*. London: David Fulton.

Gibbons, S. (2009) 'To know the world of the school and change it': An Exploration of Harold Rosen's Contribution to the Early Work of the London Association for the Teaching of English, *Changing English* 16.1, 93–101.

Creber, P. (1971) *Lost for Words*. Harmondsworth: Penguin.

Dixon, J. (1967) *Growth through English*. Oxford: Oxford University Press.

Holbrook, D. (1979) *English for Meaning*. Windsor: NFER.

Hourd, M. (1949) *The Education of the Poetic Spirit*. London: Heinemann.

Sampson, G. (1921) *English for the English*. Cambridge: Cambridge University Press.

Cliff Hodges, G. (2010) Rivers of Reading: Using Critical Incident Collages to Learn about Adolescent Readers and Their Readership, *English in Education* 44.3, 181–200.

Eaglestone, R. (1999) *Doing English: A Guide for Literature Students*. London: Routledge.

Gibson, R. (1998) *Teaching Shakespeare*. Cambridge: Cambridge University Press.

McCormick, K. (1994) *The Culture of Reading and the Teaching of English*. Manchester: Manchester University Press.

Rosenblatt, L. (1995) *Literature as Exploration*. New York: The Modern Language Association of America.

Kress, G. et al. (2005) *English in Urban Classrooms: A Multimodal Perspective on Teaching and Learning*, Ch. 3 A New Approach to Understanding School English: Multimodal Semiotics. London: RoutledgeFalmer.

Matthewman, S. (2011) *Teaching Secondary English as if the Planet Matters*. London: Routledge.

Searle, C. (1998) *None but Our Words: Critical Literacy in Classroom and Community*. Buckingham: Open University Press.

Yandell, J. (2008) Exploring Multicultural Literature: The Text, the Classroom and the World Outside, *Changing English* 15.1, 25–40.

Abbs, P. (2003) *Against the Flow: Education, the Arts and Postmodern Culture*. London: RoutledgeFalmer.

Stevens D., and McGuinn N., (2004) *The Art of Teaching Secondary English*. London: RoutledgeFalmer.

Harrison, B. (1983) *English Studies 11–18: An Arts-based Approach*. London: Hodder & Stoughton.

Fleming, M. (2010) *English Teaching in the Secondary School*, Ch. 9 Drama. London: Routledge.

Heathcote, D. (1967) Improvisation, *English in Education* 1.3; reprinted in J. N. Britton (ed.) (1984) *Teaching English: An International Exchange*. London: Heinemann.

Benton, M. (2000) *Studies in the Spectator Role: Literature, Painting and Pedagogy*. London: RoutledgeFalmer.

D'Arcy, P. (1995) *Two Contrasting Paradigms for the Teaching and Assessment of Writing*. Sheffield: NATE/NAAE.

Goodwyn, A. (1995) *English and Ability*. London: David Fulton.

Marshall, B. (2011) *Testing English: Formative and Summative Approaches to English Assessment*. London: Continuum.

Marshall, R. (2009) Epistemic Vagueness and English Assessment: Some Reflections, *English in Education* 43.1, 4–18.

Reed, M. (2004) Write or Wrong? A Sociocultural Approach to Schooled Writing, *English in Education* 38.1, 21–38.

Robinson, M. and Ellis, V. (2000) Writing in English and Responding to Writing, in J. Sefton-Green and R. Sinker (eds) *Evaluating Creativity: Making and Learning by Young People*. London: Routledge.

Allen, D. (1987) *English, Whose English?* Sheffield: NAAE.

Mittins, B. (1988) *English: Not the Naming of Parts*. Sheffield: NATE.

Myhill, D. (2011) Living Language, Live Debates: Grammar and Standard English, in J. Davison, C. Daly and J. Moss (eds) *Debates in English Teaching*. London: Routledge.

Perera, K. (1987) *Understanding Language*. Sheffield: NAAE.

Sharwood-Smith, M. (2007) British Shibboleths, in E. Ronowicz and C. Yallop (eds) *English: One Language, Different Cultures*. London: Continuum.

Rosowsky, A. (2010) Writing It in English: Script Choices among Young Multilingual Muslims in the UK, *Journal of Multilingual and Multicultural Development*, 31.2, 163–179.

Green, B. (1993) *The Insistence of the Letter: Literacy Studies and Curriculum Theorising*. London: Falmer Press.

Millard, E. (1997) *Differently Literate: Boys, Girls and the Schooling of Literacy*. London: Falmer Press.

Andrews, R. (2001) *Teaching and Learning English: A Guide to Recent Research and Its Applications*. London: Continuum.

Brice Heath, S. (2007) 'Afterword', in V. Ellis, C. Fox and B. Street (eds) *Rethinking English in Schools: Towards a New and Constructive Stage*. London: Continuum.

Daly, C. (2011) The 'Real World' of Technologies: What Kinds of Professional Development Are Needed for English Teachers?, in J. Davison, C. Daly and J. Moss (eds) *Debates in English Teaching*. London: Routledge.

Kress, G. et al. (2005) *English in Urban Classrooms*. London: RoutledgeFalmer.

Medway, P. (2010) English and Enlightenment, *Changing English* 17.1, 3–12.

Introduction

Researching for this book has been a real pleasure: revisiting books and papers on English pedagogy I had not read for some time, and discovering several new pieces and even authors. I hope readers will find similar pleasure in looking through the excerpts I have selected, and in the suggestions for critically reflective activity in each chapter. It certainly strikes me that in the ever-changing world of English in education, the *quality* of the writing at the heart of this world has been consistently very high: thoughtful, erudite, provocative and imaginative.

Having said this, I have to issue apologies. For reasons of space, I have not been able to include all the writers or texts I should have wished for, and the extracts I do include are necessarily brief. I hope those omitted – or those readers who feel they should not have been – can forgive me: there have been some difficult decisions to come to here. Where possible, I have tried to include such authors in the further reading sections that are central to the chapters, but I do understand that this is no real substitute. In terms of the brevity of each extract, it is my sincere hope that each piece may give something of the flavour of the larger text (and context) from which it derives, and lead to further, more wide-ranging, exploration – not least of the full text in question. In effect, I would regard the book as a failure if it did not whet the appetite for this larger quest.

There have also been difficult editorial decisions in deciding who goes where in the organizational structure of this reader, and I am conscious that, in this context as in so many others, boundaries and delineations are artificial and not always helpful constructs. Again, I hope readers may understand, and

1

find their own paths through the book: assuredly, the chapters and sectional divisions are not meant to separate aspects of English pedagogy, but merely to group conveniently. I have tried also to find a balance between historical and contemporary writing, with relevance to the current situation the key factor governing choice here, but with an eye also on important pedagogical themes not necessarily dominant in today's discourses. Similarly, there is some representation of international perspectives, but the tendency is towards British commentators; again, the further reading sections, I hope, point towards other, often more international, writers and texts.

The exploratory activities central to each chapter are intended to promote further, critical understanding – and the key word here is 'critical'. I invite readers, whether long-serving English teachers, student teachers or others concerned with the subject and its pedagogy, to think critically, reflectively and purposefully about the many thoughts and opinions represented here, and to relate such matters to their own professional practice and observation. The activities, in this sense, are meant merely as prompts to aid such processes: any reader worth his or her salt will inevitably go well beyond such prompts. Again, were this not to occur, I should regard the book as having fundamentally failed. English pedagogy is a journey, and journeys are best envisaged as adventures: it is in this spirit that I invite readers to explore further.

1 Theoretical models

An important part of this book's purpose is to show how theory and practice complement each other – and are in fact inseparable. Whereas the thrust of much of today's educational legislation suggests that effective teaching (and, consequently, learning) is best undertaken without much conscious acknowledgement or exploration of theoretical dimensions, I feel it is important to emphasize just how significant theory should be, not least in improving the practice of the classroom. With this in mind, the first chapter looks precisely at possible theoretical models: those based on ideas and practices pertaining to critical literacy, to the seminal work of Gunther Kress, and to other appropriate models of English pedagogy.

Part 1: Models of critical literacy

Sources

1.1 Morgan, W. (1997) *Critical Literacy in the Classroom*. London: Routledge.

1.2 Peim, N. (2009) Transformations: English, Theory and Bernstein, *Changing English* 16.2, 149–164.

1.3 Rosen, H. (1977) Out There, or Where the Masons Went, in M. Hoyles (ed.) *The Politics of Literacy*. London: Writers and Readers Publishing Cooperative.

Introduction

These extracts span over thirty years of radically critical commentary on the nature of English teaching and learning, and two continents with quite distinctive traditions and outlooks. The time span involved testifies to the continuing tradition of radically conceived literacy as a basis for English pedagogy at secondary level, and the extracts have been grouped together here to illustrate similarity of approach. Nevertheless, there are important distinctions to be made – many of which will be revisited through other views represented in subsequent chapters of this book. For Harold Rosen (1919–2008), then one of the stalwarts of English radical pedagogical development, the social context of education is fundamental – indeed, as he writes below, 'there is nothing else to talk about' – but clearly in terms of both radical critique *and* culturally grounded optimism. Twenty years later, writing from her Australian perspective, Wendy Morgan echoes the latter characteristic in subtitling her book 'the art of the possible'. Her writing offers a subtle, essentially positive, critique of modes of critical literacy as practised, especially in the Australian context. Nick Peim, in his tightly argued paper, explores some of the tensions alluded to by Rosen and Morgan from a more contemporary standpoint, drawing especially on the insights of the sociologist Basil Bernstein, and suggestive of the need for further (and genuinely liberating) subject transformation in English.

Extract 1.1

While critical literacy, like charity, begins at home and may need to unsettle the comforts of these certainties, there is enough rough correspondence between these categories and the practices of English teachers for us to proceed – with caution . . .

In my story there are four sometimes overlapping groupings, founded on different concerns: aesthetic, ethical, rhetorical or political. The aesthetic takes an often conservative approach to a bookish cultural heritage; the ethical concerns itself with the personal and literary development of readers and writers; the rhetorical has a functional emphasis on appropriate or correct expression and use of genres; and the political centres on the effects of power in texts and society. Any of these discourses can and does make authoritative claims for its truth and value according to its own founding principles, and it is indeed productive for the teachers and students who find themselves within it.

[. . .]

The fourth discourse is more radically political. An earlier stream from the 1970s, of cultural and communications studies, has now for the most part converged with the turbulent waters of critical literacy . . .

. . . [C]ultural heritage and growth discourses emphasise in different ways the educational – moral, affective and expressive – benefit to private individuals and are founded, more or less overtly, on assumptions about the shared cultural values which underpin such aesthetic-cum-moral approaches. Their ethics is one of care and government of the self. By contrast both genre and critical literacy advocates argue for an English whose ethics address the politics of differentially advantaged groups. The latter discourse however is more radically utopian in seeking nothing less than the renovation of society, while a discourse of functional grammar is compatible with a realistic accommodation to present sociopolitical arrangements. For these two any utopia is still to be achieved. For the cultural heritage a past utopia is to be reinstituted; and for a growth discourse a utopia is perhaps first to be achieved within any individual, the benefits flowing outwards in greater tolerance towards others in a society organised as at present.

Students' capabilities as instructed readers are the focus of two very different discourses, of cultural heritage and critical literacy. For despite the emphasis of the former on literary canonical texts and the attention of the latter to non-literary texts, both tend to take a defensive approach of 'inoculation' against popular culture (Buckingham and Sefton-Green 1994). Students' reading practices are regarded with more tolerance in growth and genre discourses. The former depends on a personalist and expressivist reader-response pedagogy and therefore aims to give student readers opportunities to do what comes 'naturally'. Their competence is demonstrated in responses which centre on the reader's sensibility rather than simply on textual knowledge. By contrast the focus of genre teachers' reading instruction has been to identify generic structures and features in order that students may reproduce them. However, advocates of genre teaching who also have knowledge of functional systemic linguistics will use the resources of the grammar to analyse the meanings that are 'realised' in written texts.

Different kinds of writing are privileged within different discourses: essays of literary criticism or argumentation; writer-centred, more confessional explorations of personal understanding; the production of texts which adhere to the structures – and strictures – of a generic model; or writing which supplements and challenges the sufficiency of a given model in form or substance. In each case the kind of writing required of students follows from, confirms and demonstrates the particular kind of reading competence promoted almost as much as it does their writing capabilities.

The point to be made from this schematic overview is that such discourses of English education are not entirely distinct from one another. They may be informed by somewhat similar ideologies. None is fixed and stable; through their conversations and even arguments over time they may assimilate compatible aspects of others or change by accommodating criticism from other discourses. Ultimately all are alike founded on principles of modernist education. That is, they take for granted that the deliberate interventions of education aim at the improvement of students and society, however differently each conceives of those goals. They assume that the effectiveness of teachers' professional work can be measured in the products and persons of students. And each discourse has faith that there are proper objects of study, whether these be academic disciplines or the culture at large, and that these can be adequately engaged with by rational inquiry into the meaning 'in' any text, practice and institution. (We shall see subsequently how critical literacy has attempted to engage with the radical challenges poststructuralism and postmodernism present to this educational endeavour.)

Buckingham, D. and Sefton-Green, J. (1994) *Cultural Studies goes to School: Reading and Teaching Popular Media*. London: Taylor & Francis.

Extract 1.2

Towards the end of the 1970s and in the early 1980s discourses of transformation and dissolution confronted English. They began to be discussed as alternative ways of thinking about subject identity. They offered alternatives to the core ideas, objects and activities of subject practice. These discourses came to be known under the collective name of 'theory'. Theory was a broad amalgam of discourses outside or at the edge of subject boundaries. It included elements of philosophy, linguistics, history, Cultural Studies, Media Studies and even psychoanalysis. From a broader framework of ideas, poststructuralism, postmodernism and postcolonialism offered new ways of seeing and interpreting the world. This uncertain amalgam that was 'theory' interrogated the fundamental categories of subject constitution and called them into question. The definition of English was problematized, expanded and altered. The subject dramatically discovered its histories and its ideological dimension.

Theory highlighted fundamental conditions. The given order of things in English was found to be inescapably political. The subject that dealt with representation, language and meaning could no longer be seen as politically neutral. Interrogation precipitated crisis – or so it seemed. The subject *had to* reform itself, had to find a new way of being that would answer to the troubling questions posed by theory. English teaching in schools could not remain untouched by this upheaval. Fundamental change seemed inevitable. Some hailed a new world order of language and textual studies as signifying the necessary end of English. The revolution would bring freedom from old constraints and produce new and expansive possibilities (Peim 1993). English confronted dissolution.

The promised end, however, did not occur. English in HE transformed itself, made itself if anything more eclectically contradictory. English teaching in schools drew on established routines, ideas and practices, reconstructing itself within the National Curriculum (Cox 1991). Far from declaring itself an outmoded relic of a bygone conception of education and quietly retiring from the scene, English remains at the core of the National Curriculum and robustly recruiting in Higher Education.

[. . .]

A new world order of English never arrived. The apocalypse never materialized. Some changes to subject identity occurred but hardly effected the radical displacement promised by some of the bold titles of the time. From present perspectives we can see that the present constitution of the subject has a strongly defined form. English didn't suddenly transform itself into something altogether more politically self-conscious nor did it gradually wither away. The new influx of ideas and perspectives on language and textuality offered by theory never quite took hold and certainly failed to make the drastic changes they had promised or threatened. After a brief agonistic flurry over the setting up of the National Curriculum, English in schools became established along lines that remained significantly attached to a notional standard English and to a fairly unregenerate notion of literature with a strong flavour of cultural heritage (Cox 1994). In the process the work of English teachers became more controlled. How was it that, in spite of a powerful vision of a radically transformed future, English teaching settled to its present form?

[. . .]

What Bernstein's sociology does is to identify for us the complexity of defining and locating the object of transformation. English is not simply what happens in classrooms, nor yet the determinations made in curricula and by exam institutions. There is no free-floating *essential* spirit of the subject that exists above and beyond its particular realizations in contexts of practice. English *is* also and inescapably pedagogy and pedagogical relations: and these, always already structured by relations of social and cultural difference, are caught up in often strongly contrasting orientations to meaning. These reflections may perhaps serve to prompt us to be more circumspect in our ambitions and to take a more sober view of changes in the field of educational practice. The liberalization of English was effected through changing discourses of pedagogy in the 1960s and through loosening of the examination system in the 1980s; but it was also always subject to reclamation by coding at the level of language. Liberalization was not, ever, equal to liberation. Would-be radical changes at the curriculum level driven by theory, in spite of their rational justifications, have to engage with the insulation of subject identity and how this gets imprinted into professional being. The particular form of contemporary pedagogical relations driven by the larger logic of performativity defines professional being in a very particular and strongly framed modality.

The heady moment of theory had encouraged some of us to think we could step outside social and institutional enclosures to apply a radical remedy to the social ills of curriculum and pedagogical class bias. In fact, the enclosures were always around us, ready to resist declassification and to assert their powerful framing devices all the more strongly or all the more subtly. The puncturing of the myth of progress effected by the National Curriculum and its related governmental machinery liberates English from the false promise of completed development; at the same time it problematizes subject aspirations to be the ground for a politics of education.

Peim, N. (1993) *Critical Theory and the English Teacher.* London: Routledge.
Cox, B. (1991) *Cox on Cox.* London: Hodder and Stoughton.
Cox, B. (1994) *The Battle for the English Curriculum.* London: Hodder and Stoughton.

Extract 1.3

So we are going to talk about the social context? And a good thing too. But strange. The tidy abstraction of it; a non-combative, dusted-down, orderly little phrase. What does it stand for? The little world we can look at through the window, go shopping in, take buses from, play truant in? The invisible hinterland of this morning's *Times* where I read of 'the magnification of state benefits as the major source of subsistence for unproductive members of society'? The portable 'construction of reality', the internal architecture we have built for ourselves out of our social encounters? It cannot be the ramshackle edifice of institutions, pronouncements, channels of communication, labelled strata, laws and doctrines cobbled together by history for us to scuttle about in. The social context, as we call it, is not an arena in which we perform our dramas. It is the dramas themselves; people in action with each other and against each other improvising the text as they proceed.

> 'Thus it is not language which generates what people say. Language does not possess this magical power or possesses it only fitfully and dubiously. What people say derives from praxis from the performance of tasks, from the division of labour—arises out of real actions, real struggles in the world. What they actually do, however, enters consciousness only by way of language, by being said.'

Therefore, if I am a bit needled by the phrase, 'the social context', it is because, cropping up like this, it announces that we are moving on to our next interesting theme and in due course we shall proceed to others. But that isn't it at all. Essentially, *there is nothing else to talk about*.

[. . .]

The doleful litany chanted endlessly is that the children and young people in schools are totally submerged by powerful manipulative forces outside their control which brutalize and stupefy them. If that message strikes home then it is small wonder if teachers who step forward to expose, analyse and demolish, feel in their hearts that they are puny in the face of giants who can spend more on one advertisement than one of them will spend on school books in the whole of a teaching career. Of course it is right to see and understand how such things work but the mistake is to believe that all around us are nothing but sad and spiritless victims. There are other forces at work. The miracle is not that we are all deformed by the dominant culture of our society but how much grows in the teeth of it, how our humanity asserts itself, how it asserts itself in the world of our pupils. We should not see the tabloids and commercials as the only emblems of their world, just as we should refuse to let a sanctified canon of literary works be the only alternative voice.

For there is that other assumption about society which corrodes our thinking, that the great working-class of this country with its largely unwritten history, its heroism, its self-transforming engagement with life, its stubborn refusal to be put down is nothing but a deprived inarticulate herd. Even the new radical teacher sensitive to the language of working-class pupils and armed with political theory can be corroded by the social assumptions which abound in current educational and sociological literature. We are told that working-class children cannot learn to read because they have no books in the home and their parents do not read. Transmitted deprivation I believe they call it now. Yet millions of people throughout Europe in the late nineteenth and early twentieth centuries won their way to literacy from homes which were totally illiterate.

Exploratory questions

■ What do you understand by the term 'critical literacy' in both practical and theoretical contexts?
■ In what ways do the three writers represented here complement and contrast with each other in their approaches to social contexts for English pedagogy?
■ In particular, how relevant are Rosen's 1977 view and Morgan's Australian perspective to your experience of English teaching and learning?
■ Peim especially offers a directly critical view of the current state of English teaching in schools; how does this accord with or contrast to your reflections on your own experience?
■ Although not directly concerned with English teaching, the radical Brazilian educationalist Paulo Freire (1921–1997) coined the terms 'pedagogy of hope' and 'pedagogy of critique' to encapsulate what he saw as the essential complementary characteristics of a radical education; what do you understand by these terms? How may they relate to the views expressed above?
■ The implication of all three writers' work is that what happens in schools, and particularly in English classrooms, can make a positive difference in terms of social equality; is this important to you? Do you agree?

Further reading

The writers cited below are all crucially concerned with the social and cultural dimensions of education, either explicitly linked to English pedagogy or more implicit in connection. Both Freire and Bernstein are in the latter category, and both are referred to above; the books I have selected form useful introductions to their distinctive and seminal work. Rosen and Creber were both influential during the latter half of the twentieth century, emphasizing the social contexts for literacy in the UK, while Peim, Gale and Densmore, and Glazier have each in their own way developed these perceptions and ideas. From the US perspective, Giroux has been prolific and insightful in pioneering and developing Freire's critical pedagogy: he has much to say to English teachers among others.

Bernstein, B. (1970) Education Cannot Compensate for Society, in B.R. Cosin, et al. (1971) *School and Society: A Sociological Reader*. London: Routledge & Kegan Paul.

Creber, J.W. Patrick (1972) *Lost for Words: Language and Educational Failure*. Harmondsworth: Penguin.

Freire, P. (1992; this edn 2006) *Pedagogy of Hope*. London: Continuum.

Gale, T. and Densmore, K. (2000) *Just Schooling: Explorations in the Cultural Politics of Teaching*. Buckingham: Open University Press.

Giroux, H. (1997) *Pedagogy and the Politics of Hope: Theory, Culture and Schooling*. Boulder, CO: Westview Press.

Glazier, J. (2007) Tinkering towards Socially Just Teaching: Moving from Critical Theory to Practice, *Changing English* 14.3, 375–382.

Peim, N. (1993) *Critical Theory and the English Teacher: Transforming the Subject*. London: Routledge.

Rosen, H. (1993) *Troublesome Boy: Stories and Articles by Harold Rosen*. London: English and Media Centre.

Part 2: A seminal influence: Gunther Kress

Sources

2.1 Kress, G. (1995) *Writing the Future: English and the Making of a Culture of Innovation*. Sheffield: NATE.

2.2 McGuinn, N. (2005) A Place for the Personal Voice? Gunther Kress and the English Curriculum, *Changing English* 12.2, 205–217.

Introduction

Currently Professor of English in Education at the perennially influential London University Institute of Education, Gunther Kress has had a long-standing and significant influence on English pedagogy over the past three decades. Indeed, Kress's positive impact on English pedagogy was recently honoured at the 2011 NATE National Conference: he received an award for lifetime services to English education. Much of Kress's work has centred around the social and cultural production of texts across a vast range of genres, both written and otherwise; current concepts of multi-modality owe a great deal to his pioneering research. Although the excerpt below was written almost twenty years ago, their relevance remains today, and if anything is enhanced by the more obviously multi-cultural and multi-modal contexts we find ourselves working within. However, there has also been considerable opposition to, and concern over, some aspects of Kress's work. Sometimes this has derived from misunderstanding or misconstruction: his emphasis on genre, for instance, has been misused to give spurious credibility to approaches to textual reconstruction (including of course writing) in English classrooms which seek merely to replicate generic characteristics with scant concern for value, affective subjectivity or social context (the idea that all persuasive writing must abide by 'the rule of three' is a currently prevalent example in English classrooms).

Nick McGuinn's critique, however, derives from a much more subtle reading of Kress. Himself an English teacher and teacher educator of experience and standing (and the original English Subject Officer for the nascent National Curriculum for English in the 1980s), McGuinn embraces rather different priorities within English pedagogy in taking issue with some of Kress's central tenets. In particular, McGuinn is concerned to stress a 'personal growth' model of English teaching and learning, and here reflects on the challenges he feels Kress has mounted on such a position.

Extract 2.1

To state some of my own principles quite early on: I am firmly of the opinion that everything in the new curriculum will need to be judged in terms of its effect in giving young people certain dispositions: confident in the face of difference – cultural, linguistic, ethnic, ethical – and confident in the everyday experience of change; able to see change and difference as entirely usual conditions of cultural and social life; *and* to see them as essential productive resources. My own aim is to move away from a conception of the critical reader, beholder, or commentator – away that is, from a position of *insight* which provides the ability to produce analytic critique, as the central goal of a humanistic education. Critique is an essential element of informed citizenship, and of public participation; in my envisaged future society it will be seen as an essential component in producing the new goal of *education as social action: the envisaging, design, and making of alternatives*. This ability, it seems to me, will be central to the felicitous progress of so-called post-industrial societies.

This brings me to the central principle: the social human whom I envisage through this curriculum will have been given the means of making lives which are fulfilling, have dignity, and are capable of producing happiness. These things – as the famous Monty Python sketch demonstrated ('eh you were lucky, you had a shoebox; we only had a hole in t' ground') – are historically contingent, relative. The world of tomorrow may offer its inhabitants a lesser level of material well-being, *and yet* an at least equal and perhaps greater level of satisfaction.

English is central in this task. No other subject in the curriculum has that potential, or that task; nor can I see that changing in the short-term, say over the next ten to fifteen years. It assumes some deep transformations in the subject English – in the context of a multicultural, multilingual society; in the context of globalisation and its corrosive effects on the nation-state; of technological change; and of the effects of the globalised and then re-localised media.

[. . .]

The futures which are proposed at the moment, either explicitly, implicitly, or by default, are not the only futures which can be imagined, even within (Fast) Capitalism. It is here where the English curriculum can, in its contents and resources, project a vision of another future, a 'working future'. English is the curriculum of communication and of representation, among others, and in its treatment of the practices of communication, as of the practices of representation, the texts, the visions we make, and how we make them, it holds, implicitly, the most decisive power for the making of working futures.

Extract 2.2

For someone like Kress, who is so acutely aware of an 'authoritative' discourse's capacity to demand 'our unconditional allegiance' (Rosen, 1992, p. 127), the hegemonic impulses behind a National Curriculum which declares certain literary texts worthy (and by extension, others less worthy) of inclusion in the schooled experience of the nation's young people, are of course to be contested. The issue as he sees it, however, goes much deeper than discussions about what literary text might or might not receive governmental approval. Kress would question the validity of an entire literary enterprise which foregrounds reader at the expense of text. By doing so, he issues a major challenge to champions of the personal growth model of English who might assert with John Dixon that:

> in ordering and composing situations that in some way symbolise life as we know it, we bring order and composure to our inner selves.
>
> (Dixon, 1967, p. 20)

Implicit in Kress's criticism, too, is a questioning of the validity of those 'reader response' theories which held sway in English classrooms for so many years. To assert the claims of the reader over those of the text, Kress might argue, is to uphold a position which could, at best, be viewed as self-indulgence and at worst, dangerous political naivety:

> Think of the way in which, in the field of 'cultural studies', an emphasis on analysing 'what the text says' is gradually being replaced by an emphasis on 'how different audiences read the same text', an emphasis, in other words, on the apparent freedom of interpretation which, by diverting attention away from the text itself, allows the limitations which the text imposes on this 'freedom of reading' to remain invisible, and therefore, perhaps, all the more efficacious and powerful. Or perhaps more insidiously, the transfer from 'what the text says' to 'what this theory constructs this text to be'.
>
> (Kress & van Leeuwen, 1996, pp. 26–27)

The contrast between a statement like this and Louise Rosenblatt's famous articulation of the response-theorist's credo, is stark:

> What, then, happens in the reading of a literary work? Through the medium of words, the text brings into the reader's conscious-ness certain concepts, certain sensuous experiences, certain images of things, people, actions, scenes. The special meanings and, more particularly, the submerged associations that these words and images have for the individual reader will largely determine what the work communicates to him. The reader brings to the work person-ality traits, memories of past events, present needs and preoccupa-tions, a particular mood of the moment, and a particular physical condition. These and many other elements in a never-to-be duplicated

combination determine his [sic] response to the particular contribution of the text.

(Rosenblatt, 1970, pp. 30–31)

Even as we congratulate ourselves on our ability to 'meet texts half way', to work alongside them in the construction of meanings, we are, Kress might argue, seriously missing the point—which is, bluntly, that the 'genre will construct the world for its proficient user' (Kress, 1994, p. 126).

[. . .]

This takes us to the heart of Kress's challenge to the personal growth model of English. When so many powerful genres (like the memorandum we have just explored) are at work in society, seeking to construct our world or position us in particular ways, why should we spend time in school absorbed in the study of literature or the creation of narrative fiction? To put it bluntly, if most of our adult reading and writing will be confined to the completion of tax returns, mortgage applications or shopping lists, why do we make our school children study Shakespeare or write poetry?

How many school-leavers will be called on to become 'creative' users of language? How many will be called on to become creative users of the genres which are most highly valued in the school, the 'poetic' or literary genres? One might reset the aims of language education more modestly, more realistically and more usefully to give students skills in the use and manipulation of language, to give them a fuller understanding of the manifold meanings of language and of the genres with which they will come into contact.

(Kress, 1994, p. 126)

That the National Literacy Strategy classroom is now a place where the study of literature is reduced to 'priority passages' and where the explicit investigation of language through such 'non-fictional' genres as 'recount' or 'persuasion' prevails, is testimony to the triumph of Kress's ideas.

How is a teacher still wedded to the study of literature to respond? My first, defensive, instinct was to think of Shakespeare's King Lear and cry:

O, reason not the need: our basest beggars
Are in the poorest thing superfluous:

15

Allow not nature more than nature needs,
Man's life's as cheap as beast's . . .

(*King Lear* Act II, Scene iv, ll. 261–264)

I wanted to say this because I feel, ultimately, that there is something a little bleak about Kress's position. The clue is in the recommendation, quoted above, that we might 'reset the aims of language education more modestly'. By this he suggests that we call into question the whole notion of encouraging creativity in school:

> Such a view of genre should serve to give some pause to the demands for creativity often imposed on children in school, explicitly or implicitly. The language forms, the grammar are given; the generic forms in which they join to form larger, organized and integrated wholes are also given. No single individual is likely to create a new genre. Where then exists the possibility for creativity? At what stage can creativity become a legitimate demand anyway, given that the years up to the age of fourteen at least are spent in learning the conventions? Should mastery of the conventions be sufficient?
>
> (Kress, 1994, p. 125)

Rosen, H. (1992) The Politics of Writing, in Kimberley, K., Meek, M. and Miller, J. (eds) *New Readings: Contributions to an Understanding of Literacy*. London: A&C Black.

Dixon, J. (1967) *Growth through English*. Oxford: Oxford University Press.

Kress, G. and Van Leeuwen, T. (1996) *Reading Images: The Grammar of Visual Design*. London: Routledge.

Rosenblatt, L. (1970) *Literature as Exploration*. London: Heinemann.

Kress, G. (1994) *Learning to Write* London: Routledge.

Exploratory questions

■ Kress makes great, and very specific, claims for the subject English here; do you feel these are justified, from your experience of the English classroom?

■ McGuinn, in his paper, tells us that the 'personal growth model of English . . . was the tradition into which I was inducted as a young English teacher'; does this model still have the same attraction today?

■ Is there a real conflict between the positions espoused by Kress and McGuinn here, making them mutually exclusive of one another? Or is some sort of synthesis possible?

Further reading

Further explorations of Kress's and McGuinn's work appear below, amplifying some of the points emerging from comparison of their viewpoints. Bearne and Marsh's writing is helpful in giving enhanced awareness of the issues surrounding literacy and inclusion – central in any study of English pedagogy – whilst Goodwyn and Findlay, and Davison and Moss further expand the context.

Bearne, E. and Marsh, J. (eds) (2007) *Literacy and Social Inclusion: Closing the Gap.* Stoke-on-Trent: Trentham.

Davison, J. and Moss, J. (eds) (2000) *Issues in English Teaching.* London: Routledge.

Goodwyn, A. and Findlay, K. (2002) Secondary Schools and the National Literacy Strategy, in A. Goodwyn (ed.) *Improving Literacy at KS2 and KS3.* London: Paul Chapman.

Kress, G. (1994) *Learning to Write.* London: Routledge.

McGuinn, N. (2005) Living in Contradiction without Shame: the Challenge of Intertextual Response in GCSE Poetry, *Changing English* 12.2, 24–252.

Stevens, D. and McGuinn, N. (2004) *The Art of Teaching Secondary English: Innovative and Creative Approaches.* London: RoutledgeFalmer.

Part 3: Further models: growth and critique

Sources

3.1 Dixon, J. (1967) *Growth through English.* Oxford: Oxford University Press.
3.2 Griffith, P. (1987) *Literary Theory and English Teaching.* Milton Keynes: Open University Press.

Introduction

Like Gunther Kress, John Dixon's huge contribution to the development of English pedagogy was marked at the 2011 NATE National Conference at the British Library – for lifetime services to NATE; John's response was characteristically self-effacing, but also revealed his determination to adhere to and develop the centrality of personal growth in the teaching and learning of English. Indeed, the idea of fostering personal growth in the English classroom continues to have a powerful appeal to both established and beginning English teachers – more often than not it is regarded as the definitively special role of the English teacher to pursue such an approach. The extract below is from a powerful statement of principle, appropriately entitled *Growth through English*, itself a record of and critical reflection upon the deliberations of the vitally significant Dartmouth Seminar of 1966, creatively bringing together English pedagogues from the UK and USA (later extended to allow dialogue with Canadian, Australian and New Zealand practitioners). In the years following Dartmouth, of course, ideas of personal growth were extensively challenged – indeed some of the extracts in this chapter illustrate the challenge vividly – and, often as a consequence of this challenge, were further honed. Interestingly, however, the conflict often focused on the place of literature in English teaching: the nature of the personal growth espoused frequently highlighted a response to literature as either cultural heritage, to be honoured accordingly, or cultural artifact to be critiqued alongside any other text. Writers such as Peter Griffith, whose *Literary Theory and English Teaching* appeared in 1987 (extract below), attempted to offer radical synthesis of these positions – an enterprise in which many English teachers are likely still to be engaged.

Extract 3.1

Knowledge and mastery of language

It is in the nature of language to impose system and order, to offer us sets of choices from which we must choose one way or another of building our inner world. Without that order we should never be able to start building, but there is always the danger of over-acceptance. How many teachers, even today, welcome and enjoy the power of young people to coin new words to set alongside the old order? How often do social pressures prevent us exercising our power to modify the meaning of words by improvising a new context, as in metaphor? Sometimes, it seems, our pupils are more aware than we are of the fact that language is living and changing; we could help them more often to explore and test out its new possibilities. Inevitably, though, the weight of our experience lies in a mature awareness of the possibilities and limitations raised by the more permanent forms of order in language. There has already been an explicit case (at our own level) in this chapter. The question "What is English?" invites a different form of answer from, say, "What at our best are we doing in English classes?" If we wish to describe a process, *composition* for example, the first question will tend to suggest the finished product (the marks on the page even) rather than the activity of bringing together and composing the disorder of our experience. "What . . . doing" will suggest nominal forms of verbs (bringing, composing) and thus help to keep activities in mind.

[. . .]

To sum up: language is learnt in operation, not by dummy runs. In English, pupils meet to share their encounters with life, and to do this effectively they move freely between dialogue and monologue—between talk, drama and writing; and literature, by bringing new voices into the classroom, adds to the store of shared experience. Each pupil takes from the store what he can and what he needs. In so doing he learns to use language to build his own representational world and works to make this fit reality as he experiences it. Problems with the written medium for language raise the need for a different kind of learning. But writing implies a message: the means must be associated with the end, as part of the same lesson. A pupil turns to the teacher he trusts for confirmation of his own doubts and certainties in the validity of what he has said and written; he will also turn to the class, of course, but an adult's experience counts for something. In ordering and composing situations that in some way symbolize life as we know it, we bring order and composure to our inner selves. When a pupil is steeped in language in operation we expect, as he matures, a conceptual-izing of his earlier awareness of language, and with this perhaps new insight into himself (as creator of his own world).

Extract 3.2

There was always one curious unintended outcome of what Eagleton has termed the 'left-Leavisite' position with regard to textual study. In theory it taught the Great Tradition to transmit certain core values, and it taught the study of advertisements in order to illustrate the corrupting effects of language used for base capitalist motives, which thereby corrupted the pure springs of human discrimination. In practice, though, such a method of teaching generated a powerful subjective impression in anyone graduating from it that he was now equipped to analyse *any* piece of text, no matter what its source was. This was, then, a kind of structuralist narratology *avant la lettre*, handicapped only by the absence of any real method capable of being described to a sceptic: 'Either you see it or you don't', was a response that was often uttered with more force than effect. To be able to offer pupils this sense of power over their environment seems a desirable goal, especially if the sense of power is more than a delusion and can lead in some way to an effect on the pupil's environment.

What I am in effect saying is that literary theory is about more than just literature, which in any case is an entity that it is impossible to define. Again the reader may perhaps feel that we have all trodden this way before;

after all, the lyrics of Bob Dylan were studied in class by pupils whose hair is now grey. However, I am not convinced that they were studied as aspects of a signifying process, and the use of theory, I have been suggesting, is crucial to the use of literature. To feel that you are able to say something about the workings and effects of a nineteenth-century novel, a pop lyric, a Jacobean play, a Clint Eastwood film, a Great War poem and a soap opera is a good experience; to be able to demonstrate this feeling in terms of actual practice is even better.

One move in this direction would consist of a general reassessment of those parts of the curriculum that are now beginning to be described, on school timetables as well as in volumes of theory, as aesthetics. The drive towards a co-ordinated programme of work in this area is altogether admirable but, if its effect is simply to demarcate a field in which personal expression is uniquely but temporarily privileged, then we will have seen no more than a wall of greater circumference going up around the same old ghetto. What I have in mind is something more like the old project that arose out of Saussure's original conceptions and was followed through in the early phase of structuralism: a study of the business of signification in all its aspects, with, in the original model at least, linguistics installed in the centre as the type of all communicative systems.

Linguistics cannot now be held to have this centrality since the assault of post-structuralists such as Derrida broke the bond between signifier and signified, but the study of discursive practices seems at least as capable of occupying the kind of key role I have described. It is for this reason that I would not wish to see aesthetics, in its new and broader definition, confined to dealing with nothing more than expressions of subjectivity, since this would unnecessarily separate it from the possible forms of analysis of these activities. 'English', as a curricular entity in the school curriculum, is capable of fulfilling a pivotal role between a widened aesthetics and a re-theorized social studies.

Exploratory questions

■ Although Dixon and Griffith approach English from different standpoints, both emphasize synthesis of theory and practice; consider what would characterize textual teaching in an English classroom drawing from both commentators' thoughts.

■ Does the personal growth model of English pedagogy remain central? How has it developed/might it yet develop as the broader context changes?

■ Is it really possible, or desirable, to give all texts equal weight through study? Where exactly does that leave the question of the *literary value* of a particular text? Is such a concern appropriate to English teaching, or should subjectivity of taste reign supreme?

Further reading

Richard Andrews' book is a very helpful guide to relatively recent research into English pedagogy, and in fact could accompany any of the chapters in the current reader to good effect. Dixon and Stratta, Davies, and Sedgwick, from their various angles, tackle the perennially fascinating – if elusive – question of what constitutes (or perhaps should constitute) English teaching and learning. Mark Pike's work, represented in two texts below, emphasizes the moral and spiritual dimensions of English pedagogy: highly significant, and often overlooked, aspects of the subject.

Andrews, R. (2001) *Teaching and Learning English: A Guide to Recent Research and its Applications.* London: Continuum

Davies, C. (1996) *What is English Teaching?* Milton Keynes: Open University Press.

Dixon, J. and Stratta, L. (1985) Meanings of English, in *English in Education.* Sheffield: NATE.

Pike, M. (2004) *Teaching Secondary English.* London: Paul Chapman.

Pike, M. (2011) Developing as an Ethical English Teacher: Valuing the Personal and Poetic in Professional Learning, *English in Education* 45.3, 224–235.

Sedgwick, F. (2001) *Teaching Literacy: A Creative Approach.* London: Continuum.

2

The nature and structure of the English curriculum

Chapter 2, following our brief exploration of theoretical aspects of English pedagogy, seeks to examine how the English curriculum, in practical and structural terms, defines itself – including, significantly, how theory and practice relate to each other and to structural contexts. The breadth of the subject, and its defining characteristics, is important here, as presented in both parts of the chapter, and I include a reasonably wide range of commentators to illustrate the potential for development.

Part 1: Contextual breadth

Sources

1.1 Cox, B. (1995) *Cox on the Battle for the English Curriculum*. London: Hodder & Stoughton.
1.2 Scholes, R. (1998) *The Rise and Fall of English*. New Haven, CT: Yale University Press.
1.3 West, D. (2008) Changing English, *Changing English* 15.2, 137–143.

Introduction

There is of course no clearly defined border between English as theorized and English as taught and learned in the vast range of possible educational sites and contexts; similarly, the overlap between all the chapters in the present book is often considerable, and the boundaries are often a matter of convenience rather than principle. Overlap is thus best seen as potentially fertile for new inter-relationships, and the possibilities which may arise from them, and perhaps nowhere more so than those between pedagogical theory, as introduced in Chapter 1, and curricular practicalities and structures.

The three writers (and practitioners) represented in this part are all implicitly, and creatively, aware of this dynamic relationship, and for all three there is a strong sense that theory and practice relate to each other in interesting ways. Brian Cox's influence on the development of English as a core National Curriculum subject in England and Wales has been huge: the report of his committee of enquiry into the nature and reality of English teaching, the now famed 'Cox Report' of 1989, ushered in the first National Curriculum Orders for the subject, and, despite the concerns of many in the field at the time, was generally seen as acceptable by the teaching profession. In the extract below, by way of conclusion to his book detailing the struggles of the 1990s to retain a humane core in the curriculum, Cox proposes ten key principles of English. Robert Scholes comments from a rather different vantage point: an American academic, he writes here of his concern for the apparent demise of the subject English and suggests fundamental structural changes in order to breathe new life into its teaching and learning. David West, more recently, presents his particular version of curriculum structure for English, in many ways building positively on the insights of earlier commentators like Cox and Scholes (among many others, including those featured in the present book) in favour of a radical view of literature as necessarily central.

Extract 1.1

[I]t may now be possible for teachers to reclaim the curriculum, and to teach according to good practice. The remaining large worry concerns the nature and significance of assessment in the future.

I conclude by listing ten features which should be at the centre of the post-1995 English curriculum:

- Teachers should use a variety of approaches in the teaching of reading. Teachers should develop appropriate classroom techniques, and keep abreast of the latest research.
- Pupils should be encouraged to write in a variety of forms, preparing drafts to be discussed with the teacher and their peers. They should write for real audiences, and on occasions their work should be

published in class and school magazines. High standards in handwriting and spelling are a *sine qua non*.

- Teachers themselves should write, in whatever forms please them, and when appropriate show their work to their pupils. They should act as role models.
- There should be a strong commitment to drama in the classroom, and to high standards of speaking and listening.
- All pupils should be helped to speak and write Standard English by the age of 16.
- The LINC project should be revived and funded by Government. The Cox proposals for knowledge about language, including grammar and Standard English, should be reintroduced in the classroom and properly evaluated. The value of the linguistic and cultural knowledge of bilingual children should be recognised.
- Choice of texts for reading should keep to the framework in the Cox curriculum. Texts should be chosen from a variety of genres, from works from pre-1900 English literature, including Shakespeare, and from writings in English from other cultures. Teachers should be free to choose texts they and their pupils will enjoy.
- Media texts should be studied in the classroom.
- The requirements of children with special needs should be carefully evaluated by teachers and advisers with specialist knowledge.
- A significant element of the assessment of English should be by coursework.

Extract 1.2

[W]e need only rethink what grammar, dialectic, and rhetoric might mean in modern terms. My own rethinking of these terms has taken the form of seeing all three of the trivial arts as matters of textuality, with the English language at the center of them, but noting their extension into media that are only partly linguistic.

[. . .]

My first trivial topic is grammar, traditionally the driest and narrowest of academic subjects. I propose to change all that by means of a course of study that follows the implications of the grammar of the pronouns all the way to the subject and object positions of discourse . . .

The second semester of "grammatical" study in my new trivium would treat the topic of Representation and Objectivity. Representation is an activity in which a textual subject positions someone or something else as a textual object. . . .

The last of the trivial topics I am proposing might well be taught first in any sequence of core courses, because it deals with more familiar matters and perhaps even with more immediately accessible material. I am not offering a rigid order or sequence of courses here, in any case, but trying to suggest how one might go about revitalizing the old trivium, the third division of which, you will remember, was rhetoric. I would be inclined to call a modern course in rhetoric something like Persuasion and Mediation. Such a course would obviously include the traditional arts of manipulation of audiences but would also point toward the capacities and limits of the newer media, especially those that mix verbal and visual textuality to generate effects of unprecedented power. Such a course would embrace the traditional topics of rhetoric but would extend them in certain specific directions. One might well wish to begin with Aristotle's *Rhetoric,* but in this kind of course the *Poetics* would also have a place as a discussion of both another type of manipulation and a specific medium (tragic drama) that mediates human experience in a particular way, incorporating the hegemonic codes of a particular cultural situation. . . .

. . .By putting language and textuality at the center of education, we would not be making some gesture of piety toward the medieval roots of education, but we would certainly be acknowledging the cultural past of our institutions. More important, however, we would be responding to the "linguistic turn" of so much of modern thought and to the media saturation that is the condition of our students' lives as well as of our own. Already, in such a trivium, the cultural past will have begun to be presented as a body of texts that can help students to understand their current cultural situation—just as they help their teachers (who also, of course, continue to be students). This trivium should serve, as well, to whet the appetite for other courses that attend more specifically to the historical narratives of one or another mode of cultural activity. If the pigs and the dogs learn to communicate and negotiate with one another, perhaps they can turn this flock of cultures into a nest of singing birds, and make such music as will stir the corrupting carcass of Western Civilization itself. That, at least, is my hope.

Extract 1.3

This is a plea, then, for the subject of English to go back to basics, to deal once again with the text as text, to treat the literary text first and foremost as language. This might not be easy. I attended last year's English Subject Centre conference, where I argued for the centrality of language in literary studies. 'That's all well and good,' said one university delegate, 'but no one in this room apart from you knows anything about language.' The comment was greeted with much nodding of heads. In a way, I can sympathise with that argument. I studied English to doctoral level without even knowing what a verb was, and only began learning about language through teaching English language abroad. We have come to a situation in which we have a whole generation of teachers of English at university level who know nothing about English – as a language. 'English', for most people outside the academy, means 'the English language'. It is only inside the academy that 'English' means anything but language. Of course teachers of English are in a difficult position: they would have to learn about language from scratch. But what a wonderful opportunity, and as academics we are paid to learn and to learn what is new so that we can teach our students well. English scholars over the last few decades have been willing to engage with psychology, with political science, with history, with sociology. They have tried to incorporate these disciplines into their reading of literature – often with risible results. Why, then, are they so unwilling to deal with the one phenomenon that stares them in the face every time that they open a book? Why do they immediately leap from words to world, from the language of which a text is composed to the world that the text suggests? Why does language appear so transparent to them as not to exist at all?

I am not arguing here for a boring stylistics, for a treatment of literature in which different sentence types are identified, verbs are counted and metrical feet analysed. Stylistics has come a long way from its beginnings in the early 1960s, and is now called literary linguistics or, better, cognitive rhetoric or cognitive poetics. Language, now, is seen as the manifestation of fundamental cognitive processes, and it is these cognitive processes which are common to both writers writing and readers reading. It is upon these processes that literature – both in its production and its reception – is founded, and it is upon these processes that we should therefore be focusing all our efforts. English, therefore, should be part of cognitive science. It should integrate the remarkable insights that have been developed in cognitive science since the 1960s, and should, in turn, enable cognitive science to develop new insights in the future, for what the subject of English deals with – texts that foreground and explore our most profound cognitive processes – is precisely the field of interest of cognitive scientists.

The central notion in a changed English would be that of *construal*. This notion, which is so central to cognitive science, refers to the mental processes whereby we, as a species, interact with and make sense of the world. At the heart of the notion is the idea that the external world is not simply out there to be perceived or experienced, but that our perception or experience of that world is always and inevitably mediated through the cognitive processes with which we have been endowed as a species. Thus, for example, the reason that we talk about TIME in terms of the horizontal, rather than the vertical, plane (we say *a long time* and *a short time* rather than *a tall time* and *a small time*) is because we experience motion horizontally rather than vertically. Construal is the fundamental characteristic that we have as a species; it is our *sine qua non*. It is the characteristic that is fundamental to literature, that most human of activities, too. Such a notion would unify the subject; give it a soul. What would such an English look like?

[. . .]

Scholars such as Turner and Richards argued for the subject of English to be at the very heart of the humanities; indeed, for the subject to be the *sine qua non* of any humanist education. However, it can only take its rightful place at the heart of the humanities if the subject focuses on what it is that makes it human: on literature as a peculiar linguistic phenomenon that reveals our most fundamental cognitive processes. At the moment, English concentrates upon anything but what is important, and it seeks to gain credibility and value through aligning itself with other disciplines – with history or sociology or political science or (very outdated) psychology. As a consequence, the subject has no relevance, and is rightly derided outside itself as harmless quackery. It is time that we change the subject to make it relevant and important again – the most relevant and important subject that we, as human beings, have. We can only do that by repositioning the subject within cognitive science, and exploring through the language of the literary text the complex cognitive processes involved in its creation and reception – the cognitive processes which are an intrinsic part of our everyday lives, and which find heightened and peculiar expression in that strange and wonderful entity we call literature.

Exploratory questions

- In your professional experience, how does the structure of the English curriculum – its *form*, in other words – influence its *content*?
- Which of Cox's ten recommendations, cited above, can you recognize in today's secondary English classroom? Consider further their presence or absence: are there clear reasons for either?

- The National Curriculum itself is a fairly recent phenomenon, as Cox demonstrates in his books (quoted from above, and recommended below); what are its advantages and disadvantages for the subject English?
- Considering the implications of all three of the extracts above, what are their relative merits in the context of your own professional (and personal, as a learner) experience?
- If you had the task of designing an English curriculum from scratch, what sort of broad outline might you adopt? Explore, for instance (as do the quoted writers) the place of language, literature and non-linguistic communication.

Further reading

Each of the readings below serves further to illuminate structural and formal aspects of the English curriculum, from a range of perspectives. Cox (and indeed his committee) has interesting things to say about the development of the National Curriculum for English and its relationship to broader questions of literacy, whereas Burgess et al. make an impassioned plea for a humanely critical core for any English curriculum. Knight was one of the most ardent critics of the National Curriculum, as it emerged, but his book is well worth reading, not merely as a historical position, but for its (debatable, of course) prescience.

Burgess, T., Fox, C. and Goody, J. (2002) 'When the hurly burly's done': What's Worth Fighting for in English Education. Sheffield: NATE.

Cox, B. (1991) Cox on Cox: an English Curriculum for the 1990s. London: Hodder & Stoughton.

Cox, B. (ed.) (1998) Literacy Is Not Enough. Manchester: Manchester University Press.

DES (1989) English for Ages 5–16 (The Cox Report). London: HMSO.

Knight, R. (1996) Valuing English: Reflections on the National Curriculum. London: David Fulton.

Part 2: Further structural explorations

Sources

2.1 Stevens, D. (2011) Cross-curricular Teaching and Learning in the Secondary School: English. London: Routledge.

2.2 Thomson, J. (2004) New Models of English Teaching, in W. Sawyer and E. Gold (eds) Reviewing English in the 21st Century. Melbourne: Phoenix.

2.3 Yandell, J. (2008) Mind the Gap: Test and Classroom Literacies, *English in Education* 42.1, 70–87.

Introduction

These three extracts represent different models of structural development for curricular English. In my writing about cross-curricular possibilities for English, I subtitled the book 'the centrality of language in learning', thus hoping to build on concepts of language across the curriculum first promulgated by the Bullock Committee of 1975 – *Language for Life*, or, more commonly, simply the Bullock Report (largely written by ex-HMI Ron Arnold). I was also at pains to maintain that such an approach need not imply any dilution of English; indeed, my emphasis was on enrichment of the subject through exploration in what could be possible in the English classroom. Jack Thomson, an Australian academic, seeks to build on previous models (usefully summarized by him, and by Cox in his report, cited previously) in favour of what he terms a 'rhetorical and ethical model', echoing some of the issues and possibilities highlighted in the previous part. John Yandell's approach is essentially critical of the 'test literacy' model of English teaching he feels to be so damaging to the teaching of the subject. He uses his critique skilfully as the basis for suggesting a quite different, more creative and social approach, using as his research model a 14-year-old pupil in a London comprehensive school English classroom.

Extract 2.1

. . . I am concerned in effect to develop the nature of English lessons as timetabled and clearly defined in the vast majority of secondary schools – and more or less determined by the subject-based nature of the National Curriculum – by alerting English teachers and others to the vast potential within the subject for making creative and practical use of cross-curricular ways of working and conceiving of the world in the context of English pedagogical traditions and *within English lessons*. However, I am also keenly aware that this book is one of a series considering cross-curricular teaching and learning from the perspectives of all the other secondary school subjects, and that, consequently, there will be almost inevitable overlap between some areas across the series. I view this as constructive rather than unfortunate, in that the very essence of interdisciplinary initiatives demands a broader outlook than that implied by subject boundaries. Making such connections is at the heart of this series and of this particular volume, and I would feel encouraged if, as a result of adopting cross-curricular approaches *within* English, its teachers felt inspired to seek more and more connections with colleagues from other subject disciplines in both practical and theoretical pedagogical contexts.

The combination of practice and theory is, for me, critical, in all senses of the word: the one informs the other in what I hope is a genuinely creative enterprise as outlined in this book and series. As the educational philosopher Wilfred Carr has pointed out, there has been a tendency over the past couple of decades to neglect any philosophical debate centring on the nature of education and schooling – 'education now insulates itself from philosophy . . .' as he puts it (Carr 2004: 35) – and I should like to think that in its small way, this book may contribute a little to reinvigorating the debate. For debate it has to be, especially as this entire series seeks to endorse a radical curricular turn for secondary schooling, and to ignore the issues is in effect simply to accept the status quo. Those searching simply for teaching tips on how to meet new curricular demands will be disappointed – although I invite them to read on anyway in the spirit of enquiry as to how philosophy and practice may work together in the way Griffiths has shown us: a

> practical philosophy . . . [that] is interested in the empirical world as a way of grounding its conclusions in interaction between thinking and action . . . Theory is brought into question by the experience it questions, and is then used to inform practical actions.
>
> (Griffiths 2003: 21)

With this in mind, I shall be drawing upon a number of relevant (I hope) commentators – some familiar from mainstream educational thought, others perhaps less so – as guides for our enterprise.

My own professional record as teacher of English in several comprehensive schools, in two as Head of English, and over the past fourteen years as a teacher educator in English, within the Durham University Post Graduate Certificate in Education (PGCE) course, has led me increasingly to question any rigid adherence to subject delineation. Every year, the PGCE English group at Durham comprises excellent beginning teachers from a wide range of subject specialisms alongside English itself (whatever that term now means, given its own healthy diversity), including, at various times, sociology, media studies, communications, law, modern languages and drama. My own first degree was in Humanities, involving arts, philosophy and humanities modules alongside English itself, and subsequent study has explored further interdisciplinary connections, within the arts field particularly. I am also interested in intercultural connections in the teaching and learning of English, drawing on both the Romantic tradition central to that subject's history, and on perspectives of critical pedagogy through the work of Freire, Giroux and others; I hope the possible syntheses between diverse approaches to teaching and learning will inform and illuminate the interdisciplinary project at the heart of the series. In schools I was particularly keen to foster links with arts, humanities and languages colleagues, and I have attempted to continue and develop this collaborative breadth of approach across these subjects (especially art, music and drama) at teacher education level. For example I, and a few willing colleagues, frequently begin the PGCE course by asking our students, across up to four subject areas, to work in cross-curricular small groups scouring the local area for resourceful teaching and learning connections based on a sense of the place. In part of course this is simply to get people to work together – but then this is important too. I have also been positively alerted to the possibilities of adopting and adapting scientific and mathematical pedagogical approaches for English – a challenge, certainly, but often an illuminating one.

The nature of the curricular subject English, particularly as it appears in the secondary school curriculum, is one characterised by paradox. Something about the subject has ensured that it has been, and remains, at the sharp edge of curricular battles – with both defeats and victories recorded – over the years since its invention as a core subject (some would say, *the* core subject) around the turn of the nineteenth into twentieth century. As Peel maintains in his helpful discussion on the nature of the subject English (Peel *et al.* 2000: 22), its 'most universal quality is diversity'. In the context of the present exploration, focusing on the cross-curricular, interdisciplinary nature and potential of secondary school subjects, English again, predictably enough, has an especially vital role to play, and one almost defined by paradox. On the one hand, the distinctive nature of the subject is fiercely contested, with particular positions regarding its nature defended vociferously; on the other hand, the sometimes startling, often bewildering breadth, and the arguably amorphous quality of English, lead many to conceive of it as the cross-curricular subject par excellence. Effectively, in this book I attempt to argue for a new kind of English teacher: an interdisciplinary English teacher, aware of the breadth of the subject and the interconnectivities involved (the *inter* of 'interdisciplinary', which is why I prefer the term to 'cross-curricular'), but also especially conscious of *language*, in all its textual diversity, as the sharp focus. Certainly few throughout the world of education would disagree that a secure grasp of language and its qualities lies at the heart of effective teaching and learning – and this is the very stuff, the defining characteristic, of English in the curriculum.

Carr, W. (2004) Philosophy and Education, in Carr, W. (ed.) *The RoutledgeFalmer Reader in Philosophy of Education*. London: RoutledgeFalmer.

Griffiths, M. (2003) *Action for Social Justice in Education: Fairly Different*. Maidenhead: Open University Press.

Peel, R., Patterson, A. and Gerlach, J. (2000) *Questions of English*. London: RoutledgeFalmer.

Extract 2.2

A new model, then, might well be called a 'rhetorical' and ethical model, or even a Rhetorical, Ethical, Sociocultural, Political model, as it is a RESPonsible model, on behalf of, or REPresenting human agency. Richard Andrews uses the term 'rhetorical', by which he means that students should learn to use all of the rhetorics of their culture with some expertise to operate in – and on – their world as choice-making human beings (Andrews 1994; 1995). I would add to Andrews' comments an additional emphasis on helping students to understand the values involved in all aspects of their work in English, and the need, when making choices, to understand the ethical implications and consequences of such choices.

Such a *rhetorical/ethical model involves personal growth as well as a full awareness of the relationship between language and power, a familiarity with social practices and their discourses, and an understanding of the political and ideological formation of texts and of matters of values and ethics*.

In considering the issue of values and ethics, my approved model of English teaching, unlike the 'cultural studies' or 'textuality' model, recognises that some texts are more complex and profound than others, even more humane and 'life-promoting' to use F.R. Leavis's term without endorsing the rest of his program. Ultimately, I believe we need to help our students to develop the skills and understandings to be able to make hierarchical value judgments that some texts are linguistically, stylistically, aesthetically, psychologically and/or philosophically more significant – and better – than others, while recognising that such judgments are partially culturally constructed. I would emphasise the point that in helping students to develop the literary – and literacy – abilities to make such judgments, we want these judgments to be made by students themselves and not to be imposed on them by teachers (or by media commentators, politicians, or other community leaders). In such circumstances there will be many different, even conflicting, value judgments made in any classroom.

Further, the more students know about the linguistic, historical and cultural construction of reality and subjectivity, the less they are likely to be fully determined human beings. As Pam Gilbert has said, 'By fostering in our students a genuinely critical stance towards language and its discursive formations, we foster "producers" not "consumers": active participants rather than passive recipients' (Gilbert 1987, p. 249).

Ethical teaching practices

Obvious examples of ethical practices for teachers are to make sure they:

- don't teach one reading practice as if it were the only way to read (as happened to my generation at Sydney University, when New Criticism was in vogue, and assumed to be not so much the preferred model of reading as the only one)
- don't impose their own value judgments on students, but are honest about their preferences, when asked. (In other words, they shouldn't replace any traditional canon with one of their own.)
- do teach students all of the reading practices available in the community, so that the same student can read the same text in multiple ways, and choose a preferred reading, in the full knowledge that what is chosen is partial and relative, and constructed from one's own experience, cultural knowledge, value system and historical–cultural positioning
- do help students to recognise and respect the point of view of other readers whose preferred interpretations arise from different repertoires (of experience, cultural knowledge, values and historical–cultural positioning), so that all come to understand sympathetically the perspectives offered from different cultural positionings
- do help students to understand that cultural difference is to be respected – in language use as well as in (inevitably ideological) reading practices – and that such differences are not hierarchical or to be treated as deficits

In a rhetorical/ethical model, which sets a critical approach to the reading and writing of texts in a political context, students are invited to start to challenge and question their world. In order to take an active role in shaping their future world they need to develop rhetorical skills; to become active producers of their own knowledge and skills; to learn to take responsibility for their own learning; to come to understand themselves in relation to others; to learn to cooperate with other people to solve problems; to make choices about what they do; to make decisions; and to understand and make informed, responsible and tolerant judgments about issues of values and ethics.

[. . .]

A rhetorical/ethical model is designed to give students from disadvantaged groups a powerful literacy and access to mainstream culture, with all of the choices that such access entails. It is also designed to ensure that the socially advantaged and culturally dominant groups develop the same powerful literacy and choices as their social location would lead them to assume as their normal life expectation. It is a model which involves all students in learning to work together cooperatively to solve problems and in coming to understand other people and their beliefs, while, at the same time, developing an understanding of the social origins of such beliefs. It is a model designed to help all students to live ethically in a plural but increasingly tolerant society, where difference is respected and valued. It is a model designed to problematise the current theory of 'economic rationalism' which is itself a contradictory text in a liberal-humanist society. Economic rationalism, which has, of course, driven the political and economic policies of Australian governments for the past 20 years, assumes that people need increasing material rewards to work conscientiously and assumes a view of human behaviour as being inherently motivated by greed, selfishness and fear.

Andrews, R. (1994) Towards a New Model: a Rhetorical Perspective, in Watson, K. (ed.) *English Teaching in Perspective*. Sydney: St Clair Press.

Andrews, R. (1995) *Rebirth of Rhetoric*. London: Routledge.

Gilbert, P. (1987) 'Post reader-response: the deconstructive technique' in Corcoran, B. and Evans, E. (eds) *Readers, Texts, Teachers*. Upper Montclair, NJ: Boynton/Cook.

Extract 2.3

Introduction

In July 2001, the President of the United States met a group of children from a primary school in Hackney, East London. Mr Bush listened while his wife read a story. He then commented on the importance of literacy: 'You teach a child to read, and he or her will be able to pass a literacy test' (*Times Educational Supplement*, 24 August 2001). It is intriguing that the leader of the most powerful nation on earth has such a circular view of literacy, what it is and what it is for. Children are taught to read so that they can pass a test which, presumably, is designed to assess whether they can read.

George Bush's model – that learning to read is important because one is thereby enabled to pass a literacy test – would have made perfect sense to felons in medieval and early modern England, when a member of the clergy could not be condemned to death for a first capital offence. Instead, he was branded on the hand or thumb – M for murder, T for theft. He could, however, be executed if convicted of a second offence. This 'benefit of clergy' was extended, in certain contexts, to anyone who could read, including, in the 18th century, women. The courts determined whether the accused was literate or not by giving him or her a reading test. The test passage was usually the first verse of Psalm 51:

Have mercy upon me, oh God, according to thy loving kindness; according unto the multitude of thy tender mercies, blot out my transgressions.

Many people learned the passage, known as the 'neck verse', by heart whilst in jail and, thus, were able to read the passage when on trial. Some references to this practice suggest that the condemned men or women were not actually reading, that the act of committing the verse to memory was, in effect, cheating. Not having undergone the prescribed course in phonics, they were pretending to read (but not actually reading). But, as George Bush understands, they had indeed learned to read – they were functionally literate. Functional illiteracy, for them, would have had a simple consequence: hanging.

Neck verse literacy shares three key features with George Bush's literacy: it assumes a simple binary opposition of literacy and illiteracy (pass/fail or hanged/not hanged); it can easily be tested; it is the property of the individual (Bush's 'he or her'). Modern literacy tests, of course, are more sophisticated, the assessments more finely calibrated, and the outcomes more nuanced; but the underlying assumptions about literacy have more in common with the neck verse than might be imagined.

[. . .]

Whereas reading and writing in the examination are resolutely individual and monomodal pursuits, in Maeve's classroom texts are explored collectively, over time, in and through an ensemble of multimodal resources. Something of this has already been suggested by the glimpse into the class's involvement in the production of improvised scenarii. Students talked about, analysed and annotated still images derived from a wide range of productions of the play. They watched, discussed and compared two film versions, starring Olivier (1955) and McKellen (1995); they recapped and predicted and argued and questioned; they read the script – and they talked about it. Their experience of reading *Richard III* involved the reading of still and moving images, DVDs and the Cambridge School Shakespeare edition of the play, unrehearsed readings and rehearsed improvisations.

Exploratory questions

■ Peter Abbs warned that a cross-curricular model could lead to the English teacher becoming 'like a man carrying a bag of tools but with only other people's jobs to do'. How does this accord with your own experience and views?

■ Following this, what do you feel is distinctive about the subject English?

■ How far has English teaching and learning followed Thomson's 'rhetorical and ethical model'? Should it?

■ From your own professional and observational experience, is there a gap between test and classroom literacies, as Yandell maintains? If so, how may this gap be healed?

Further reading

Peter Abbs's approach, in these essays, is in favour of an arts-based model of English – we shall meet him again in this context – but he also has important critical insights into alternative structural positions. The Bullock Report has historical significance, but is also suggestive of wide-ranging and imaginative ways of bringing language to life: it remains a seminal work, albeit much neglected in the officially sanctioned models of curricular English that have followed it. Opposing any reductionist models of English and literacy, Colin Lankshear has been tireless in proposing quite different approaches, in many ways echoing Yandell's insights, noted above.

Abbs, P. (1976) *Root and Blossom: Essays on the Philosophy, Practice and Politics of English Teaching.* London: Heinemann.

DES (1975) *A Language for Life* (the Bullock Report). London: HMSO.

Lankshear, C. (1993) Curriculum as Literacy: Reading and Writing in 'New Times', in B. Green (ed.) *The Insistence of the Letter: Literacy Studies and Curriculum Theorising.* London: Falmer Press.

Lankshear, C. (ed.) (1997) *Changing Literacies.* Buckingham: Open University Press.

3 Historical perspectives

The history of the subject English is fascinating in itself, reminding us that, like any other cultural artefact, English pedagogy is constantly in flux: forming and re-forming as its contexts change, and simultaneously playing a part in changing those very contexts. As well as this (I hope) inherent fascination with the subject's recent history – and its entire history only spans a century and half or so – such study may be instrumentally important in helping practitioners avoid some of the mistakes of the past and in finding ways to build on what has been positively accomplished.

Part 1: The tradition delineated

Sources

1.1 Eagleton, T. (1983) *Literary Theory: an Introduction*, Ch. 1 The Rise of English. London: Blackwell
1.2 Knight, R. (1996) *Valuing English*. London: David Fulton.
1.3 Gibbons, S. (2009) 'To know the world of the school and change it': An Exploration of Harold Rosen's Contribution to the Early Work of the London Association for the Teaching of English, *Changing English* 16.1, 93–101.

Introduction

In a sense, of course, a single tradition of English pedagogy does not exist: indeed, a compilation of extracts such as the present volume demonstrates the diversity of viewpoints and practices at issue here. It's also true to say that the sheer complexity of the development of the subject English and its attendant pedagogies precludes a straightforward delineation. Nevertheless, at the risk of over simplification, it is important that some historical perspective is presented and appreciated; all the writers cited in this chapter testify to complexity and diversity, whilst also attempting to show with clarity and perceptiveness how English has come to be the subject it is today. In Part 1, we look at this history from a contemporary perspective. Terry Eagleton, in his hugely influential and often sardonic *Literary Theory: An Introduction*, devoted his first chapter, as entitled, to 'the rise of English': his particular brand of socialist critique of the historical processes involved are plain to see. Roger Knight pursues a rather different critical path – his standpoint is one embedded in the radical liberal humanism often at the heart of English peda- gogy as he at once celebrates Newbolt's influence on early twentieth century developments, and criticizes what came after. More recently, Simon Gibbons has conducted illuminating research into the development of English teaching and learning through the London Association for the Teaching of English (later a crucial element within NATE), and especially into the profoundly radical work of Harold Rosen.

Extract 1.1

To speak of 'literature and ideology' as two separate phenomena which can be interrelated is, as I hope to have shown, in one sense quite unnecessary. Literature, in the meaning of the word we have inherited, *is* an ideology. It has the most intimate relations to questions of social power. But if the reader is still unconvinced, the narrative of what happened to literature in the later nineteenth century might prove a little more persuasive.

If one were asked to provide a single explanation for the growth of English studies in the later nineteenth century, one could do worse than reply: 'the failure of religion'. By the mid-Victorian period, this traditionally reliable, immensely powerful ideological form was in deep trouble. It was no longer winning the hearts and minds of the masses, and under the twin impacts of scientific discovery and social change its previous unquestioned dominance was in danger of evaporating. This was particularly worrying for the Victorian ruling class, because religion is for all kinds of reasons an extremely effective form of ideological control. Like all successful ideologies, it works much less by explicit concepts or formulated doctrines than by image, symbol, habit, ritual and mythology. It is affective and experiential, entwining itself with the deepest unconscious roots of the human subject; and any social ideology which is unable to engage with such deep-seated a-rational fears and needs, as T. S. Eliot knew, is unlikely to survive very long. . . .

[. . .]

Fortunately, however, another, remarkably similar discourse lay to hand: English literature. . . . The key figure here is Matthew Arnold, always preternaturally sensitive to the needs of his social class, and engagingly candid about being so. The urgent social need, as Arnold recognizes, is to 'Hellenize' or cultivate the philistine middle class, who have proved unable to underpin their political and economic power with a suitably rich and subtle ideology. This can be done by transfusing into them something of the traditional style of the aristocracy, who as Arnold shrewdly perceives are ceasing to be the dominant class in England, but who have something of the ideological wherewithal to lend a hand to their middle-class masters. State-established schools, by linking the middle class to 'the best culture of their nation', will confer on them 'a greatness and a noble spirit, which the tone of these classes is not of itself at present adequate to impart'.

The true beauty of this manoeuvre, however, lies in the effect it will have in controlling and incorporating the working class:

> It is of itself a serious calamity for a nation that its tone of feeling and grandeur of spirit should be lowered or dulled. But the calamity appears far more serious still when we consider that the middle classes, remaining as they are now, with their narrow, harsh, unintelligent, and unattractive spirit and culture, will almost certainly fail to mould or assimilate the masses below them, whose sympathies are at the present moment actually wider and more liberal than theirs. They arrive, these masses, eager to enter into possession of the world, to gain a more vivid sense of their own life and activity. In this their irrepressible development, their natural educators and initiators are those immediately above them, the middle classes. If these classes cannot win their sympathy or give them their direction, society is in danger of falling into anarchy.

Arnold is refreshingly unhypocritical: there is no feeble pretence that the education of the working class is to be conducted chiefly for their own benefit, or that his concern with their spiritual condition is, in one of his own most cherished terms, in the least 'disinterested'. In the even more disarmingly candid words of a twentieth-century proponent of this view: 'Deny to working-class children any common share in the immaterial, and presently they will grow into the men who demand with menaces a communism of the material.' If the masses are not thrown a few novels, they may react by throwing up a few barricades.

Literature was in several ways a suitable candidate for this ideological enterprise. As a liberal, 'humanizing' pursuit, it could provide a potent antidote to political bigotry and ideological extremism. Since literature, as we know, deals in universal human values rather than in such historical trivia as civil wars, the oppression of women or the dispossession of the English peasantry, it could serve to place in cosmic perspective the petty demands of working people for decent living conditions or greater control over their own lives, and might even with luck come to render them oblivious of such issues in their high-minded contemplation of eternal truths and beauties. . . .

[. . .]

The working class was not the only oppressed layer of Victorian society at whom 'English' was specifically beamed. English literature, reflected a Royal Commission witness in 1877, might be considered a suitable subject for 'women . . . and the second- and third-rate men who [. . .] become schoolmasters.' The 'softening' and 'humanizing' effects of English, terms recurrently used by its early proponents, are within the existing ideological stereotypes of gender clearly feminine. The rise of English in England ran parallel to the gradual, grudging admission of women to the institutions of higher education; and since English was an untaxing sort of affair, concerned with the finer feelings rather than with the more virile topics of *bona fide* academic 'disciplines', it seemed a convenient sort of non-subject to palm off on the ladies, who were in any case excluded from science and the professions. Sir Arthur Quiller Couch, first Professor of English at Cambridge University, would open with the word 'Gentlemen' lectures addressed to a hall filled largely with women. Though modern male lecturers may have changed their manners, the ideological conditions which make English a popular University subject for women to read have not.

Extract 1.2

It is easy to forget that the penetration of technical and materialist vocabularies into every area of public life is of fairly recent origin. Its very success makes it seem natural. As Donald Davie has said, we are all 'subject to a daily and hourly bombardment of language from innumerable sources which characteristically . . . transform human or moral transactions into technological or financial or behaviouristic terms' (Greenbaum (Ed.),

1985). It would be surprising if education were to remain immune to those vocabularies and the modes of thinking they reflect. 'The machinery of education', said F.R. Leavis, 'works in with the modern world' (Leavis and Thompson, 1933). It is an irony of the present time that as education (with 'English' as part of it) has become more centralized the public language which it draws on and consolidates has grown increasingly eccentric. Both Arnold and Leavis, in their reminders that 'mind and spirit' cannot be accommodated within – but can be traduced by – materialist vocabularies, represent a widespread consciousness of what is at stake. However, a full half-century after *Culture and Anarchy* a government-appointed committee on the teaching of 'English' could still avail itself unselfconsciously of a public language that would have met with Arnold's approval. Like the linguist quoted earlier, the Newbolt Committee had views on 'language' 'environment' and 'control'. The differences, though, are radical. What lay to hand or, more precisely, what bound the members of that committee, was a language of conviction: a language that drew its strength and its persuasive force from a set of inherited and attested assumptions about the moral importance of a language and its literature in the life of a nation:

> English is not merely the medium of our thought, it is the very stuff and process of it. It is itself the English mind, the element in which we live and work. In its full sense it connotes not merely acquaintance with a certain number of terms, or the power of spelling these terms correctly and arranging them without gross mistakes. It connotes the discovery of the world by the first and most direct way open to us, and the discovery of ourselves in our native environment. And as our discoveries become successively wider, deeper, and subtler, so should our control of the instrument which shapes our thought become more complete and exquisite, up to the limit of artistic skill. For the writing of English is essentially an art, and the effect of English literature in education is the effect of an art upon the development of human character.
>
> (HMSO, 1921, p.20)

There, Newbolt speaks out of the powerful tradition of understanding to which it is indebted for its confident tones. 'Environment' tends nowadays to be used in a purely material sense. With Newbolt, however, it is a word that embraces both the inner and the outer worlds. Language is the chief way in which the two are united, the chief way in which we inhabit the world into which we are born. We have no choice in that respect. We live and work in a native language from which we cannot escape; it shapes our thoughts and feelings, places limits on our understanding. Thus – and this is Newbolt's most important point – the quality of our thoughts and feelings, the depth of our understanding, will be very much a matter of the quality and depth of the language we experience. Certain conclusions for the teaching and learning of English inevitably follow. Newbolt speaks of

> . . . English in the highest sense, that it is the channel of *formative culture* for all English people, and the medium of the creative art by which all English writers of distinction, whether poets, historians, philosophers or men of science, have secured for us the power of *realising* some part of their own experience of life.
>
> (HMSO, 1921, p.12)

The use of the word 'realise' here is crucial and clarifies the nature of those 'discoveries' of which the first passage quoted speaks with such forceful conviction. In 'realising some part of their own experience of life', we make it more probable that we shall be able to 'realise our own impressions and communicate them to others'. The culture of which those writers are a part will thus be formative: our range of feeling, our sensibility, will be the richer for their influence. None of Newbolt's key words is open to precise definition; the appeal is, implicitly, to experience.

Greenbaum, S. (ed.) (1985) *The English Language Today*. Oxford: Pergamon Press.
HMSO (1921) *The Teaching of English in England*. London: HMSO.
Leavis, F. R. and Thompson, D. (1933) *Culture and the Environment*. London: Chatto and Windus.

Extract 1.3

How far is it possible to know someone through what they have left, rather than through the person himself? What I know of Harold Rosen comes through his writing, the written records of his spoken word, and the memories of those who worked with him. Whether that constitutes knowledge or not on my part is perhaps unimportant. What I believe is important is the inspiration offered to me as a teacher, in the work I have encountered. In the last fifteen years it has been increasingly easy to throw one's hands in the air, express frustration at the lunatic policies of successive governments and ministers for education, whilst simultaneously declaring that all power has been moved to the centre and as teachers we no longer have any influence on the direction that schooling is being driven. The more I discover of the LATE story, of the ways in which – albeit in differing circumstances – colleagues collaborated to effect change, the more I feel it is a betrayal to do anything other than to continue to argue about, and to fight for, what I believe English should offer to children. Within that story, I think it is impossible to overestimate the importance of Harold Rosen. It is very clear from the records that the London Board really did not want to entertain the challenge to the status quo that the LATE Alternative 'O' Level was presenting, and that it would use its power to suppress this movement; it is absolutely true to say that I draw personal inspiration from re-reading the notes of that 1952 meeting and hearing the defiance in Harold's voice, fired by a commitment to a fair and just system for children and teachers.

But there is more than personal inspiration to be drawn from an account of Harold Rosen's work with LATE, and therefore reasons why the story should have resonance for the profession today. If we are to believe the rhetoric, then the current administration is interested in returning some areas of control to the teaching profession: the new National Curriculum suggests this, and the most recent changes in the assessment regime offer the promise of more autonomy in the wake of the demise of secondary national testing. There is, too, with the development of a Council for Subject Associations, a suggestion of recognition of the importance of such groups in the development of curriculum, pedagogy and assessment and in the professional development of teachers. The LATE story is one of teachers and academics working together in an apparently non-hierarchical, collaborative way to promote research-based proposals for change; if we are at a time of change we might do worse than look back at the ways in which LATE organised its work as a model for the future. And within the framework of a successful subject community or network, Harold's role seems to be a critical one to observe; someone more than prepared to do the 'donkey work', ensuring that the wheels of the collaborative machine continued to turn, but equally prepared to stand above the group to make the critical comment when needed. He was someone who, even in his earliest years in the profession, was able to work on a level footing with both academics and teachers.

And it is in Harold's contributions to the work of LATE that we see those central elements of his work that must serve as his enduring legacy. I've said my first encounter with Harold's work was through *Language, the Learner and the School*, and the beginnings of that work are clear in a strand that runs right back to the early 1950s; when, still, schools in general seem unable to develop the kinds of cross curricular language policies that were even given a reawakening by the National Strategies it is important to revisit the foundations of that work, rather than simply accept that it's a good idea but very difficult in practice, as seems to have been the case.

Running through the archives are Harold's repeated calls for the experience of the child to be at the centre of schooling and the centre of English; he is not a lone voice here, but his voice is without doubt powerful and convincing and political. At a time when we are being bombarded with words like 'personalisation' it makes sense to return to the sentiment that English work should be 'rooted in the concerns, hopes and fears, and daily lives of the pupils'. This is surely where true personalisation lies, and this is a long way from the kinds of individual target setting and intensive support that form the small print of the government's agenda. When reading Harold's words and comments, one really does feel – to coin a phrase – that 'every child matters'.

And on that note, it's perhaps important to re-emphasise that among the voices that come to life in the LATE archive, Harold's is perhaps the most overtly political, the one that most clearly alludes to issues of class, control and power. When, in 1963, LATE debated the conflicting ideas about the desired organisation and structure of the newly proposed National Association, there was clearly some disagreement about how best to ensure that a national body might have both a significant influence yet also be representative of its membership. Harold's view, recorded at the meeting, was that 'if we want to have power at the centre and function democratically, the centre must grow out of existing groups' (LATE 1963). In some ways I see this as in tune with the view I've formed of Harold's concept of English, students, teachers and classrooms: empowering students through a validation of their language, culture and experience brings a strength to the classroom; enabling teachers to share concerns and work together enables the prospect of genuine progress.

Harold felt it was a continuously necessary process to 'know the world of the school and change it'; that seems to be no less true today than when he said it over half a century ago. If all those in the English community – teachers and taught – were loyal to this sentiment then not only would it be a fitting tribute to Harold Rosen's life and work, it might actually improve children's experience.

LATE (1963) *Report of meeting to discuss formation of national association.* LATE Archive.

Exploratory questions

- Eagleton's approach to the early history of English, as exemplified in the extract above, is distinctly Marxist; how else might you interpret such developments? Explore other possible theoretical lenses.

- Knight's approach comes from quite a different direction, but is also radical in its own way: do you find this view more or less appropriate to your professional practice and ideas?

- Rosen, as presented by Gibbons, could be said to espouse the 'London' view of pedagogy, as opposed to the essentially Leavisite 'Cambridge' view held by Knight and others; which do you find more congenial?

- As a professional practitioner, to what extent do you feel it important to be aware of the history of the subject?

- How, in your own professional experience and observation, has the history of English pedagogy actually influenced current practice, and the issues and tensions involved?

Part 2: Further significant historical figures

Sources

2.1 Creber, P. (1971) *Lost for Words*. Harmondsworth: Penguin.
2.2 Dixon, J. (1967) *Growth through English*. Oxford: Oxford University Press.
2.3 Holbrook, D. (1979) *English for Meaning*. Windsor: NFER.
2.4 Hourd, M. (1949) *The Education of the Poetic Spirit*. London: Heinemann.
2.5 Sampson, G. (1921) *English for the English*. Cambridge: Cambridge University Press.

Introduction

Each of these five writers has, in his or her own way, contributed a great deal to our understanding of English pedagogy over the best part of the last century, although the list is far from definitive, and many other key writers and practitioners are represented elsewhere in this book. George Sampson, loosely representing the 'Cambridge' tradition and a determining influence on the Newbolt Report, shows even in this brief extract, the tension (recognized clearly by Eagleton and others) between humanely liberal educational values on the one hand, and the desire to ward off significantly radical or revolutionary social upheaval on the other. Marjorie Hourd, less well known (there may of course be a feminist issue here), is similarly concerned with humane pedagogy, focusing, in the Romantic tradition so important to the development of the subject English, on the teaching and learning of poetry. The personal growth model of English, likewise stemming from the Romantic outlook, is the prime focus of James Dixon's influential *Growth through English* (please see p. 17 for a fuller extract in a different context), whereas Paddy Creber, roughly contemporary, shows a deep-seated concern for the role of language in educational success or failure – increasingly close to the professional lives of English teachers. Finally, David Holbrook shows clearly his sense of language awareness at the heart of English, radically developing the Leavisite model as indeed he did throughout his career as English teacher in secondary modern schools (those schools attended by children who had failed the 11-plus examination) and as teacher educator.

Extract 2.1

Teachers examining a concept such as *comprehension*, for example, might discover its different interpretation by different specialisms. This would force them to look at more specific skills, and also to decide which should have priority, at what age or ability level, in which area of study. Are there times when we may be satisfied with a vague 'awareness', or do we require a positive response by the pupil? If so, how personal and individual may this be – would a poem be an acceptable response from a pupil engaged in a geographical study of a strand-line, for example? If this is not 'factual' enough, are we rejecting it in favour of a response which makes a fumbling attempt to replicate our own perceptions? We may of course want not fact but something like *guesswork*, and the place of deduction and inference may be usefully discussed with colleagues in other disciplines.

This example serves to emphasize the extent to which thinking about teaching objectives means thinking about *language in context*. We cannot long engage in such study, however, without facing the importance of objectives which have more to do with social behaviour than with conventional academic aims. . . .

[. . .]

If one accepts that improvement in language-use is an aim appropriate to a much wider sector of the curriculum than the five or six periods which the timetable designates 'English', the progress towards self-evaluation of the kind described may be seen to have equally wide relevance. In most subjects little attention has been paid to it, however. This is certainly true in English, where the recent emphasis has been upon 'creative' expression while follow-up processes of evaluation and improvement have been neglected. This is partly the result of uncertainty; the desire to avoid the old errors of that teacher's role which Andrew Wilkinson satirized as 'the teacher as printer's reader' – a lynx-eyed error-detector – this desire has been praiseworthy but it has left a vacuum – how do I mark it if not out of ten? The answer seems clear – hand part of the responsibility for evaluation over to the pupil, or to the group. The process begins when we encourage them simply to look at each other's work.

This is by no means as pie-eyed as it may seem. In general the idea of workshop – as a fluid and flexible teaching environment, one activity leading naturally to another – has gained ground since the Anglo-American Seminar at Dartmouth. A corollary of this idea must be that the workshop is a place where the *crafts* of language are played with, enjoyed, experimented with and, later, *analysed*. Such self-analysis is a natural part of the work of a 'creative' author; it is also something towards which we need to work in our encouragement of self-expression. Robertson cited the case of a child in the second year who spent *as much time* reading and re-working her poems as in writing them. Once the basic situation – cooperative discussion leading to revision – has been set up, the teacher will find ample opportunity to introduce all the *teaching* he could wish for. More than this, he will probably discover that technical concepts can challenge the child and renew rather than dampen motivation.

Extract 2.2

It is in the nature of language to impose system and order, to offer us sets of choices from which we must choose one way or another of building our inner world. Without that order we should never be able to start building, but there is always the danger of over-acceptance. How many teachers, even today, welcome and enjoy the power of young people to coin new words to set alongside the old order? How often do social pressures prevent us exercising our power to modify the meaning of words by improvising a new context, as in metaphor? Sometimes, it seems, our pupils are more aware than we are of the fact that language is living and changing; we could help them more often to explore and test out its new possibilities. Inevitably, though, the weight of our experience lies in a mature awareness of the possibilities and limitations raised by the more permanent forms of order in language. . . .

[. . .]

. . . For if we teachers encourage a pupil to conceptualize, we should ideally be doing this at the point where the demands at the operational level of language have already given our pupil the sense that conceptualizing is needed. As experienced teachers we should see this demand emerging and be ready to help it on the way. In other words, our knowledge of the route ahead is not something to impose on the student—thus robbing him of the delight of discovery and maybe dissociating such discoveries as he does make from the systematic framework he "received" from us.

[. . .]

. . . For, of all the representational systems, language is the best fitted to make a running commentary on experience, to "look at life with all the vulnerability, honesty and penetration [we] can command". In an English classroom as we envisage it, pupils and teacher combine to keep alert to all that is challenging, new, uncertain and even painful in experience. Refusing to accept the comfortable stereotypes, stock responses and perfunctory arguments that deaden our sensitivity to people and situations, they work together to keep language alive and in so doing to enrich and diversify personal growth.

To sum up: language is learnt in operation, not by dummy runs. In English, pupils meet to share their encounters with life, and to do this effectively they move freely between dialogue and monologue—between talk, drama and writing; and literature, by bringing new voices into the classroom, adds to the store of shared experience. Each pupil takes from the store what he can and what he needs. In so doing he learns to use language to build his own representational world and works to make this fit reality as he experiences it. Problems with the written medium for language raise the need for a different kind of learning. But writing implies a message: the means must be associated with the end, as part of the same lesson. A pupil turns to the teacher he trusts for confirmation of his own doubts and certainties in the validity of what he has said and written; he will also turn to the class, of course, but an adult's experience counts for something. In ordering and composing situations that in some way symbolize life as we know it, we bring order and composure to our inner selves. When a pupil is steeped in language in operation we expect, as he matures, a conceptualizing of his earlier awareness of language, and with this perhaps new insight into himself (as creator of his own world).

Extract 2.3

So English is a discipline of thought: and it has to do with language as the expression of 'whole' experience – that is, all our existential reality. It deals not only with ideas that can be taken and abstracted from our minds, but our bodily feelings, and emotions, our dreams, our unconscious fantasies, our creative powers, and our hopes for tomorrow. So it is a phenomeno-logical discipline, concerned with the phenomena of consciousness. Thus it is inadequate to regard English, as linguisticians and the 'language men' do, merely as a discipline of 'language use'. We have only to utter a word, or even make a silent sign, such as a wink or a pointed finger, to point *beyond* the word or sign, and express a meaning which involves the self and the other, our own body and the world, the individual dynamic psyche and a tradition of culture: the whole being-in-the-world, in time. Any symbol involves many tacit elements deep within us, even feelings in our body life, and our protensions – that is, expectancies in the flux of time, towards ever-opening possibilities and goals towards which we are drawn. English has to do with *meaning*, and 'meaning is an intention of the mind' (Husserl).

[. . .]

To get our perspective right, then, we need to see English in the wider prospect of those humanities disciplines by which we seek the truth of the world – *including* the sciences.

English is a humanities subject which is obliged to grope towards the truth, in the spirit of Husserl's injunctions to us, to pick up the original impulse in our civilization, and to pursue *something in which to believe*.

Some critics, like Bernard Bergonzi, have criticized F.R. Leavis for trying to make English a 'religion'. But this is to misrepresent the emphasis. English has to do with the pursuit of meaning through symbolism. In the pursuit of Winnicott's two questions, 'What is it to be human?', 'What is the point of life?', the first question belongs to the attempt to redefine man in answer to Kant's last question, 'What is man?'; the second obliges us to continue to assert that we *can* find meaning – as Shakespeare did, even, or not least, at the end of such a terrible confrontation with man's fate as *King Lear*; or the author of the *Book of Job* when confronting tragic despair. English *is* a 'religious' subject insofar as it *must* concern itself with these questions. It is also a creative subject, in which the dynamics of the individual are actually trained, to encourage the individual to explore his own authenticity, and to enrich and foster his effective relationship with others and the world. In this sense, it is a philosophical discipline in the existentialist sense: that is, it is involved in the development of attitudes to life. It is a *moral* discipline, since it engages inevitably with values, because these are bound up with meaning: and it changes us as we study and work.

So, English is for meaning – but not the meaning of words as the philosopher approaches them, in his concern with logic and definition nor is it analytical in the linguist's way, attending to form and structure. The use of words in English is a discipline of meaning in what I shall call a phenomenological way – as a way of understanding what goes on in the human consciousness.

Any genuine investigation of the phenomena of education must recognize that it is rooted in tacit processes; must recognize that what happens in the classroom or university lecture room is a process that depends upon intersubjectivity and subsidiary energies of 'being' including love and 'encounter'.

Extract 2.4

Good teaching has always rested upon two kinds of understanding, an appreciation of the intrinsic values of the material to be taught and a knowledge of the nature of children. But this reconciliation of child and grownup values is not always achieved in educational practice. At one time the accent was more on the adult's standard, but to-day we are experiencing a movement towards the child-centred school. Two main factors account for the swing of the pendulum: the rapid advance of psychological theory in relation to child development and the desire of a revolutionary society to liberate itself from hide-bound classical traditions. But in spite of these tendencies it is difficult to find in the majority of schools to-day a settled faith in any direction.

It is so easy to become infected with the prevailing educational jargon without an assimilation of the fundamental philosophy which gave rise to it. For example, much work goes on in some quarters under the banner of 'activity methods' which fails to reach the essential needs of individual children, whilst often in the service of the 'interest' much distortion of intrinsic values takes place. Blake's tiger stands in danger of losing its symbolic power to become part of a project centred on the jungle! The younger child is often compelled to live in a world of postmen and steam engines, 'as though his whole vocation were endless imitation'; and the older boy or girl may similarly be driven into a study of coal and transport. This is not intended as an out-of-hand attack on 'the centre of interest' method of teaching, which has done so much to eliminate dead formalism and to seek for a principle of integration within the curriculum. It is however a challenge to educationists to think what they are doing and not to accept child nature as determined by a method which can so soon become stereotyped, and not to sacrifice too easily the standards inherent in the often despised 'subjects'. It is true that the breaking-down of the subject barriers has helped to reveal the inter-relatedness of knowledge, and this has been a progressive move of the utmost importance. But there is a danger that the method may obscure its purpose, which was to discover and not to predict children's interests.

Extract 2.5

Upon the foundation of a sound education in English any future fabric of art, language, science, philosophy, commerce or mechanics can be firmly erected. Without that foundation nothing can be firmly erected. Once more I beg the reader not to confuse education with the acquisition of knowledge, of which a man may have much and still be uneducated. A boy goes to school, not to get a final stock of information, but to learn how he may go on learning, and to learn that going on is worth while. A humane education has no material end in view. It aims at making men, not machines; it aims at giving every human creature the fullest development possible to it. Its cardinal doctrine is 'the right of every human soul to enter, unhindered except by the limitation of its own powers and desires, into the full spiritual heritage of the race'. It aims at giving 'the philosophic temper, the gentle judgment, the interest in knowledge and beauty for their own sake' that mark the harmoniously developed man. Humanism is a matter of life, not of a living. . . . We want the educated boy to rise; but we want him to rise above himself, not above somebody else. If we teach the village boy to read for himself and think for himself, if we give him, not mere instruction or information, but the ability to take a view of things and share in man's spiritual heritage, it is not because we want him to grow up into the village squire, but because we want him to walk

in glory and in joy
Following his plough, along the mountain side.

The beginnings of a humane education here advocated will not involve a domestic revolution, or a rearrangement of the social system, or a new scale of moral values, or a preference of one sort of -ocracy or -ism to any other, or an upheaval of any sort. A humane education is a possession in which rich and poor can be equal without disturbance to their material possessions. In a sense it means the abolition of poverty, for can a man be poor who possesses so much? And we can begin this new world tomorrow if we wish. Let us abandon the view that humanism has to be sought in Rome or in Athens. Here, or nowhere, is our Athens.

Exploratory questions

- How far are Sampson's concerns, both positively and perhaps more negatively, still relevant for today's educators?
- The teaching of poetry is quite different today from what it was in Hourd's time, for better or for worse: from your own professional experience, does she still have pertinent things to say about the nature of English teaching? Are we indeed still concerned with the education of the poetic spirit in any meaningful way? Should we be?
- Following on from your appraisal of Hourd's relevance, what do you make of Dixon's insistence on 'growth through English'? Is it in fact this sense that makes English a distinctive curriculum subject, unlike any other?
- Creber subtitled his *Lost for Words*, from which the extract above is taken, 'language and educational failure'; how pertinent is his formulation nowadays? Is it the English teacher's responsibility to ensure that language learning, if need be right across the curriculum, leads rather to educational success?
- English is presented by Holbrook 'as a way of understanding what goes on in the human consciousness'; is this too grand a claim? Consider the question in relation to what you see and hear in the contemporary English classroom.

Further reading

Some of the writers selected below are concerned specifically with the nature and scope of English pedagogy – indeed, some are featured elsewhere in the present book. Douglas Barnes, James Britton, Caldwell Cook, Paddy Creber, Aidan Chambers (noted primarily as an author of children's and young people's fiction), John Dixon, David Holbrook, Leslie Stratta, Fred Inglis, Margaret Mathieson and Gordon Pradl, from a range of perspectives and within various contexts, have all had seminal influence on the development of the subject English. I have included John Dewey and John Holt in the list for different reasons: both have written more about the general philosophy of education, but both have things to say that are directly pertinent to the nature of English and its teaching and learning.

Barnes, D. (1976) *From Communication to Curriculum*. Harmondsworth: Penguin.

Barnes, D., Britton, J. and Rosen, H. (1969) *Language, the Learner and the School*. Harmondsworth: Penguin.

Britton, J. (1972) *Language and Learning*. Harmondsworth: Penguin.

Britton, J. (1982) *Prospect and Retrospect: Selected Essays of James Britton*, ed. G. Pradl. London: Heinemann.

Chambers, A. (1985) *Tell Me: Children, Reading and Talk*. Stroud: Thimble Press.

Cook, H. C. (1917) *The Play Way*. London: Heinemann.

Creber, J.W. Patrick (1990) *Thinking through English*. Milton Keynes: Open University Press.

Dewey, J. (1938; this edn 1997) *Experience and Education*. New York: Touchstone.

Dixon, J. and Stratta, L. (1985) Meanings of English, in *English in Education*. Sheffield: NATE.

HMSO (1921) *The Teaching of English in England* (the Newbolt Report). London: HMSO.

Holbrook, D. (1961) *English for Maturity: English in the Secondary School*. Cambridge: Cambridge University Press.

Holt, J. (1972) *Freedom and Beyond*. Harmondsworth: Penguin.

Inglis, F. (1987) The Condition of English in England, *English in Education* 21.3, 10–20.

Mathieson, M. (1975) *The Preachers of Culture: A Study of English and its Teachers*. London: George Allen & Unwin.

4

Texts and intertextuality in the English classroom

One of the rare areas for agreement among English teachers and academics concerns the centrality of texts. However, the consensus appears to stop there: what constitutes a text, how English teachers should approach them, how far we should stray from purely written texts, and the relationship between textual study and other facets of the English classroom – speaking, listening and writing, for example – are just some of the potentially divisive aspects of this field. The nine writers represented by extracts in this chapter all have particular interests and approaches to suggest, often quite controversially and challengingly. Despite this clear disparity, there is a unifying sense that texts matter: indeed, textual study may be seen as the core of English pedagogy. Further, English teachers need to be adventurous in actively (and of course theoretically) considering new and diverse texts and teaching ideas, and different approaches certainly need not necessarily be seen as mutually exclusive.

Part 1: The nature of literature and its reading in the English classroom

Sources

1.1 Cliff Hodges, G. (2010) Rivers of Reading: Using Critical Incident Collages to Learn about Adolescent Readers and Their Readership, *English in Education* 44.3, 181–200.

1.2 Eaglestone, R. (1999) *Doing English: A Guide for Literature Students.* London: Routledge.

1.3 Gibson, R. (1998) *Teaching Shakespeare*. Cambridge: Cambridge University Press.

1.4 McCormick, K. (1994) *The Culture of Reading and the Teaching of English*. Manchester: Manchester University Press.

1.5 Rosenblatt, L. (1995) *Literature as Exploration*. New York: The Modern Language Association of America.

Introduction

Part 1 is concerned with literary texts and their reading in the English classroom, including the vexed question of how English teachers should approach the 'canon'. Robert Eaglestone addresses this perennially controversial aspect of teaching texts in English: the place of the canon, and its implications for the classroom. In this context, Shakespeare is arguably the definitively canonical author, and Rex Gibson, greatly influential in fostering active, often drama-based, approaches to teaching Shakespeare, addresses the considerable issues involved here. Kathleen McCormick looks at different models of reading in practice, an under-emphasised area of the curriculum, while Gabrielle Cliff Hodges considers a particular, critical incident based approach to encouraging pupils' reading. Louise Rosenblatt's seminal work, aptly entitled *Literature as Exploration*, first published in 1938 and substantially revised for the 1995 edition, presents an utterly sane, holistic and eminently teachable vision of literature in education, and in other contexts: her work remains powerfully apposite today.

Extract 1.1

A theorist whose work influenced my thinking is Doreen Massey, especially her book *For space* (Massey 2005). In it, she draws on a range of fields such as cultural geography, philosophy and social theory. She is not overtly concerned with theories of *reading* but her ideas seem to me to have the potential to illuminate this whole area. I was interested in drawing on her thinking about time as integral to her conception of space to see whether, when applied to the reading process, it could offer fresh perspectives and hence different ways of construing readers and readership. In one of the 'ruminations' with which *For space* opens, Massey uses the example of Hernan Cortes's voyage of discovery and conquest of the Aztecs to argue that we tend to view such an enterprise as involving people travelling across space and acquiring new territory, with space represented as 'like a surface;

continuous and given' (*ibid.* p. 4). The narrative emphasis falls on the trajectories of the European explorers not the Aztecs' histories; the trajectories of the Aztecs and how *they* have come to be where they are, are absent from the picture. If, however, we reconceptualise conquest as encounter, as a 'meeting-up of histories' (*ibid.*), space acquires another dimension: time. Here, and wherever else there has been a tendency to view history or development as a single queue, with some further advanced along it than others, Massey now argues for a complete mind-shift, one in which space is seen as being formed by a multiplicity of trajectories. Those trajectories are arranged not chronologically but contemporaneously, having different origins and possibly different futures but, for the present moment, coexisting. Space is the sphere created by the interrelations and interactions of these trajectories. It is 'predicated upon the existence of plurality' (*ibid.* p. 9). Above all:

> . . . *it is always in the process of being made. It is never finished; never closed. Perhaps we could imagine space as a simultaneity of stories-so-far.*
>
> (*ibid.*)

One political implication for research of redescribing space in this way is the need to move away from the tendency to essentialise people, for example along class, gender or geopolitical lines. If space is dynamic not static it cannot be seen as an enclosure into which people may be corralled. On the contrary, it is formed more democratically by continuous encounters between differing trajectories, themselves always in transformation with the potential to change and be changed. Although a democratic imperative likewise informs sociocultural research, Massey's spatial perspectives mean attending to temporal and historical aspects of human interaction as well, not simply the here-and-now, and allows – potentially – a more open-ended prospect.

A case study of a whole class and the young readers within it offered an interesting context within which to apply some of these ideas. However, I also needed to design research methods in keeping with the sociocultural and interplay between them. I used four research methods overall to generate data including semi-structured small group interviews I conducted with the students, individual semi-structured interviews carried out by the students themselves with a parent or grandparent, and students' reading journal entries during their reading of a self-selected book. Firstly, however, the students were asked to create a collage to chart critical incidents in their personal reading histories to encourage them to reflect on sociocultural and spatial aspects of their reading. It is this collage-making activity I focus on here, why and how it was set up, some of the data it generated and its methodological value in the context of the overall project. Before turning to the collages, though, I outline briefly how existing research has tended to represent readers in their early teenage years, providing evidence for my argument that we need different research methods to try and achieve a better understanding of the complexity of their reading."

Massey, D. (2005) *For Space*. London: Sage.

Extract 1.2

The canon is still with us today. It is deeply woven into the fabric not just of English as a subject but into all forms of culture. TV and film adaptations tend to be of 'canonical' novels; publishers print 'classics'; to count as educated you are supposed to have read a smattering of 'canonical novels'. Why is the canon such a powerful idea?

First, the canon is a reflection that English always has a social *context* and could never be done in a vacuum. The canon represents the meeting point between (1) judgements of the artistic (or *aesthetic*) value of a text, and (2) the presupposition and interests, either implicit or explicit, of those who make those judgements and have the power to enforce them. What makes the issue difficult is that, despite claims to be 'objective' or 'neutral', it is very, very hard to separate out an artistic or aesthetic judgement from a judgement based on position and interests. These two are interwoven.

Second, the canon is *self-perpetuating*. In English at all levels, the same canonical texts come up again and again, year after year. A person who studied English and has become a teacher often teaches the texts she or he was taught, in part because she or he was taught that these texts were the most important. As students, you expect to study texts you have heard of and assume are worthwhile and, of course, resources that support your study, such as websites, IT resources, guidebooks or videos of productions, concentrate on canonical texts, which in a way makes them easier to study. (After all, why would a company produce a guidebook to a novel that only a few people have heard of?) Many textbooks for English and books on literature in general assume a familiarity with the canon, which also underlines its centrality. In fact, textbooks from earlier in the twentieth century were often made up literally of lists and descriptions of great books. A more recent version of this is *The Western Canon* from 1994, by the American critic Harold Bloom. This book is a long defence of the idea of the canon, and ends with a list of the thousand books (he thinks) everyone 'cultured' should have read. The canon, then, is the list of books you expect to study when you do English, and reading the canon is doing English. The subject and the canon in part define each other.

However, even those who make and publish actual lists of 'great books' admit that sometimes the lists can change, as certain books come into and out of favour. But the third reason the canon is so powerful is that it *creates the criteria by which texts are judged*. It sounds like common sense to say that the texts you study must be of 'high quality' and worthy of 'serious consideration', but these sort of statements give no sort of yardstick to measure this; the values that make a work substantial and give it 'quality' are not revealed. New or redis-covered texts are judged by the canon's standards. This means that even when, for example, AS and A2 exam boards choose books from a wider selection of texts than normal, they will probably first ask if the books have 'universal significance', 'positive values' or 'human significance'. Saying that a new novel fits the canon because it 'has' these, reaffirms the idea that an older novel 'had' them too. Paradoxically, the canon is not broken up, but reaffirmed.

The fourth reason the canon remains powerful is that it is involved with the senses of *identity* to which countries and groups aspire, and with the struggle to define identities. As the history of the canon suggested, its development was tied in with the development of ideas about nationality. It is for this reason that Toni Morrison (b. 1931), the Nobel prize-winning American author, wrote in 1989 that

> Canon building is empire building. Canon defence is national defence. Canon debate, whatever the terrain, nature and range (of criticism, of history, of the history of knowledge, of the definition of language, the universality of aesthetic principles, the sociology of art, the humanist imagination) is the clash of cultures. And *all* the interests are vested.

Because it is canonical texts that are taught, studied, examined, published, sold, bought, performed, made into TV mini-series, adapted for YouTube parodies, updated into contemporary settings in films and for bestsellers and so on, the canon plays a significant role in creating a sense of shared culture and of collective national identity. Deciding which texts are in the canon is all part of deciding who we are and how we want to see ourselves, and a threat to the canon is a threat to national identity. But does the person creating your course ask how you want to see yourself? As Toni Morrison says, all the interests are vested.

Extract 1.3

Teaching is a professional activity in which each teacher makes considered judgements to decide what is appropriate for each particular class of students. Professionals do not seek a universal recipe, a sequenced series of steps to be followed slavishly and exactly. The professional teacher's skill lies in the subtle and thoughtful adaptation of content and method to suit the actual circumstances and the unique nature of his or her own students. The many practical examples in this book are offered in the knowledge that teachers will adapt them in ways suitable for their own classrooms.

One reason why Shakespeare's plays have proved so popular for so long is their infinite capacity for adaptation. As society changes, so do the meanings and significances found in the plays. For 400 years the plays have been interpreted and performed in an astonishing variety of ways. Just as the same play can be performed very differently, so it can be taught and experienced in very different forms. A Shakespeare script is a blueprint from which actors and directors construct their vision of the play. Similarly, teachers and students respond to its multiple possibilities.

Each play works on many levels. It has a surface and a deep structure, literal and metaphoric meanings, naturalistic and symbolic potentialities and so on. Shakespeare can be studied through story and character, themes and issues, language, drama and theatre. As Chapter 3 shows, a Shakespeare play also lends itself to a host of intellectual or ideological concerns. Approaches and interpretations can take different forms and focus: political, historical, gender, psychoanalytic, aesthetic, moral. Each teacher's view of Shakespeare will play a large part in determining the nature of their students' experience and perception.

The commitment of this book is to active methods of teaching Shakespeare. Shakespeare was essentially a man of theatre who intended his words to be spoken and acted out on stage. It is in that context of dramatic realisation that the plays are most appropriately understood and experienced. The consequence for teaching is clear: treat the plays as plays, for imaginative enactment in all kinds of different ways.

Active methods comprise a wide range of expressive, creative and physical activities. They recognise that Shakespeare wrote his plays for performance, and that his scripts are completed by enactment of some kind. The dramatic context demands classroom practices that are the antithesis of methods in which students sit passively, without intellectual or emotional engagement. Shakespeare is not a museum exhibit with a large 'Do Not Touch' label, but a living force inviting active, imaginative creation. Active methods release students' imagination and involve them in speaking and acting. Such action gives focus and substance to the discussion, writing and design work that students undertake. It enables students to gain a sense of theatre and drama in their classroom. It helps them to make Shakespeare their own, as they inhabit the imaginative worlds of the plays through action. Direct experience of Shakespeare's language allows students to feel its distinctive forms and rhythms, and to respond with a real sense of personal engagement. Active methods dissolve the traditional oppositions of analysis and imagination, intellect and emotion. They encourage informed personal responses which are both critical and appreciative. In active work, students combine critical thought with empathy, confidence with a willingness to suspend judgement. Interpretations do not have to be of the narrowing 'either . . . or' type but can be the more expansive and imaginative 'both . . . and' variety.

[. . .]

Shakespeare wrote his plays to be performed, to be brought to life on stage before an audience. Over centuries, however, generations of scholars have transformed each play into a literary text. That legacy of textual scholarship has weighed heavily on school Shakespeare. It is part of a tradition that is deeply suspicious of enjoyment, that finds it hard to accept that pleasure and learning can go hand in hand. It sees literature as 'serious' and 'work', and drama as merely 'play'.

The notion of 'text' is deeply ingrained in Shakespearian study at all levels, and carries greater status than 'script'. 'Text' implies a desk-bound student who passively reads, rather than enacts the play; it implies authority, reverence, certainty. That implication does its own sad work in schools – it tacitly suggests that studying Shakespeare involves the pursuit of a 'right answer'.

In the clearest contrast, treating a Shakespeare play as a script (and calling it so) suggests a provisionality and incompleteness that anticipates and requires imaginative, dramatic enactment for completion. A script declares that it is to be played with, explored, actively and imaginatively brought to life by acting out. A text makes no such demand. Its privileged taken-for-grantedness conceals its social construction behind a mask of naturalness.

The textual approach is evident in those scholarly editions of the plays which until very recently served as models for school editions. The lengthy academic introductions and extensive footnotes encouraged school editions to mimic, inappropriately, the procedures and apparatus of university scholarship. Such editions promote teaching methods that explain and analyse, rather than enable students actively to inhabit the imaginative worlds that Shakespeare offers. This criticism in no way devalues traditional scholarship. But scholarly editions were not written for school and college students, and their academic approach is unsuited to the classroom. The scholarly model may be suitable for postgraduate study, but it has had a demotivating effect on generations of school and college students.

Extract 1.4

Whether or not they are conscious of it, however, teachers at all levels are always teaching their students how to read. The different ways students are asked to read imply particular values and beliefs about the nature of texts, the nature of readers as subjects of texts and as subjects in the world, and about meaning and language itself. Yet the dominant ideological significa-tion of reading often works against students' developing the capacity to think 'critically' about what they read, as many national assessments have demonstrated. As one possible solution to this apparent absence of 'critical reading', students need to learn to locate the texts they read, as well as themselves as reading subjects, within larger social contexts; in short, they need to be able to inquire into and understand the interconnectedness of social conditions and the reading and writing practices of a culture.

To translate such goals into the classroom, however, one needs first to have a clearly articulated theory of readers as social subjects. Men and women are neither fully determined by the culture of which they are a part nor simply individuals who can become 'free' of the dominant ideologies of that culture; rather, we are all, as Graeme Turner puts it, balanced between social determination and autonomy (132). From such a perspec-tive, one needs to recognize and communicate to students that they are both *interdiscourses*, the products of the various competing and often contra-dictory discourses that permeate their culture (Morley, 1980b, 164), and also *agents*, capable, not of transcending these discourses, but of negoti-ating, resisting, and taking action within them. Second, one needs to have a well-articulated theory of textuality that sees a text not as a container of truth or universal significance, but as something produced under specific material conditions and repeatedly reproduced (and perhaps strikingly re-written) by different readers – including students – in different conditions. In short, texts must be regarded as what Tony Bennett and Janet Woollacott term 'texts-in-use' (265), that is, products of 'the concrete and varying, historically specific functions and effects which accrue to 'the text' as a result of the different determinations to which it is subjected during the history of its appropriation' (Bennett, 1979, 148). Thus, those different textual 'functions and effects' cannot be seen simply as the result of individual, personal interpretive acts, but rather, like texts and readers themselves, they need to be placed in larger cultural contexts so that their particular consequences and alliances can be analysed. Finally, once such re-theorizing has been established, one has to develop new pedagogical practices – a subject that will be the focus of much of this book.

In the past two decades, work in literary and cultural studies – most particularly in Britain and latterly in America – has accomplished such re-theorizing of the reading subject and the text, but such work has only just begun to be translated into concrete pedagogies. By entering into more active dialogue with other areas of reading which focus more specifically on pedagogy, literary and cultural studies can begin to locate reading within the complex cultural contexts in which it actually occurs.

[. . .]

. . . The first approach is a *cognitive*, information-processing model which contends that readers must actively draw on their prior knowledge to be able to process texts. I will argue that while this approach is rooted in a relatively narrow objectivist tradition and takes as its goal the development of a model for how readers 'comprehend' texts, its insights about the ways readers construct meanings from texts have the potential to undermine this objectivist model and are compatible with a much more culturally-oriented sense of the reading process. The pedagogical practices that develop from this model, however, have not yet realized this potential.

The second approach follows an *expressivist* model which privileges the reader and the reader's life experience in the reading process. In this section, I will include various psycholinguistic approaches to teaching reading, particularly that of Frank Smith, as well as certain reader-response approaches to the reading of literature, such as those of Louise Rosenblatt, Stanley Fish, David Bleich, and Norman Holland. I will argue that while this model is perceived by many teachers as a viable alternative to the cognitive model, it cannot seriously challenge it since it lacks a theory of the text that can replace the commonsensical objectivist theory. Further, I will contend that while its student-centred pedagogy does offer a powerful alternative to the 'direct instruction' that tends to dominate the cognitive model, because the theory of the subject underlying that pedagogy focuses solely on the individual, it is vulnerable to attacks from the right and the left about its not preparing students to act in 'the real world'. Finally, the impact of this model is necessarily limited because it has been largely relegated to the teaching of literature.

The third approach I term a *social-cultural* model; it is one that privileges the cultural context in which reading occurs. Under the rubric of the social-cultural, I will include work done by ethnographers and historians in the field of literacy such as Shirley Brice Heath, Lauren and Daniel Resnick, and Suzanne de Castell and Allan Luke, and the work of radical pedagogues in the field of education who follow Paulo Freire, such as Henry Giroux and Ira Shor. While this approach is often thought of as politically 'radical', much of what it argues in fact carries out the broader social implications of the earlier two positions. It constitutes the most powerful challenge to the objectivist model, but I argue that it often does not spell out its theories of the reader- and text-in-culture in sufficient detail to support the development of truly alternative pedagogies. I then go on to argue for a theory of reading which draws on some aspects of all three approaches within a more systematic context of cultural production.

These three approaches are not diametrically opposed to each other: rather, they exist in dialectical relationship. Each acknowledges the importance of the reader, the text, and the larger social context in the reading situation, but each assigns quite different significations to the terms. While my discussion throughout privileges the social–cultural model, I am not arguing for the wholesale takeover of the other models by this model, but rather for the active development of genuine dialogue among all approaches.

Bennett, T. and Woollacott, J (1988) *Bond and Beyond*. London: Macmillan.
Bennett, T. (1979) *Formalism and Marxism*. London: Methuen.
Morley, D. (1980) Texts, Readers, Subjects, in Hall (ed.) *Culture, Media, Language*. London: BFI.
Turner, G. (1990) *British Cultural Studies: An Introduction*. Boston: Unwin Hyman.

Extract 1.5

I have used the terms *transaction* and *transactional* to emphasize the essentiality of both reader and text, in contrast to other theories that make one or the other determinate. *Interaction*, the term generally used, suggests two distinct entities acting on each other, like two billiard balls. *Transaction* lacks such mechanistic overtones and permits emphasis on the to-and-fro, spiraling, nonlinear, continuously reciprocal influence of reader and text in the making of meaning. The meaning—the poem—"happens" during the transaction between the reader and the signs on the page.

But a poem will not actually result unless the reader performs in a certain way. When "reader response" took on the dimensions of a movement, I found it necessary to underline the distinctive view of the reading process on which this book rests. The reader is recognized not only as active but also as carrying on certain different processes in nonliterary and literary transactions with the text. Both cognitive and affective elements are present in all reading. The differing amounts of attention accorded these aspects constitute a continuum ranging from predominatly nonliterary to predominantly literary.

To abstract the information or the directions for action needed after reading a sociological essay or a medical report, for example, the reader must focus attention primarily on the impersonal, publicly verifiable aspects of what the words evoke and must subordinate or push into the fringes of consciousness the affective aspects. I term this *efferent* reading, from the Latin *efferre* 'to carry away.'

To produce a poem or play, the reader must broaden the scope of attention to include the personal, affective aura and associations surrounding the words evoked and must focus on—experience, live through—the moods, scenes, situations being created during the transaction. I term this *aesthetic* reading. (This shift of attention is so essential, so much taken for granted and ignored, that usually only its effects are noted. Imagine a physiologist explaining the workings of the human body but failing to mention the essential breathing in and out of air.)

These stances are not opposites but form a continuum of possible transactions with a text. According to different purposes, readings of the same text may fall at different points on the efferent-aesthetic continuum, on different "mixes" of attention to public and private aspects. Much of our reading falls in the middle of the continuum, hence the need to adopt an appropriate selective stance. Traditional teaching—and testing—methods often confuse the student by implicitly fostering a nonliterary, efferent approach when the actual purpose is presumably an aesthetic reading.

Exploratory questions

- How and why texts are selected for the English classroom is of crucial significance for the teaching of the subject, and has wide-ranging implications; consider the practicalities from your own professional perspective – what factors are involved in the choices made?

■ Apart from its obvious representation in the National Curriculum and official examination specifications, how important is the teaching of the 'canon'? Who is effectively involved in deciding what texts are canonical?

■ Gibson makes a strong case for the inclusion of Shakespeare; do you agree? On what grounds? Would it really matter if pupils left school unacquainted with Shakespeare's work?

■ Consider your own classroom experience in the light of Cliff Hodges' paper; have there been 'critical incidents' in furthering your pupils' understanding and enjoyment of reading? What form might these have taken?

■ What do you consider to be the threats, in today's curriculum and practice, to Rosenblatt's conception of literature teaching and learning *as exploration*? Are there ways to circumvent such threats?

Part 2: Radical and critical approaches

Sources

2.1 Kress, G. et al. (2005) *English in Urban Classrooms: A Multimodal Perspective on Teaching and Learning*, Ch. 3 A New Approach to Understanding School English: Multimodal Semiotics. London: RoutledgeFalmer.

2.2 Matthewman, S. (2011) *Teaching Secondary English as if the Planet Matters*. London: Routledge.

2.3 Searle, C. (1998) *None but Our Words: Critical Literacy in Classroom and Community*. Buckingham: Open University Press.

2.4 Yandell, J. (2008) Exploring Multicultural Literature: The Text, the Classroom and the World Outside, *Changing English* 15.1, 25–40.

Introduction

In this part I invite you to consider textuality in critical educational contexts. In contrasting ways, but with a similarly radical agenda at heart, Chris Searle, Gunther Kress and colleagues, and John Yandell examine the role of textuality in the English classroom – its teaching and learning – from distinctly radical perspectives, in urban, multi-cultural classrooms.

Sasha Matthewman's book signals a relatively new direction for English pedagogy: a concern for ecological issues and environmental sustainability. Texts about human relationships to the natural world are frequently taught in

English classrooms but often with scant regard for the ecology of the world represented. Eco-criticism, as this kind of critical outlook has become known, has gained a great deal of significance in recent years, as reflected in the new National Curriculum's concern for sustainability and the considerable scope for cross-curricular teaching and learning. But whereas this entire curricular area has been generally felt to be within the domain of the humanities and sciences, Matthewman makes it clear – sometimes quite provocatively – that the subject English can play a telling, and very specific, role in highlighting the relationship between language, literature and concern for the environment.

Extract 2.1

Multimodality is based on the assumption that meaning is made through the many means (we call these modes) that a culture has shaped for that purpose; and we think that these are used to fashion the meanings of English curriculum and pedagogy no less than elsewhere, even if this is achieved differently. However, we are clear that we need to set such descriptions and analyses within theories of social explanation in the way begun in the previous chapter.

We think it is most useful to start straightaway with a demonstration of our methodology; on the one hand it shows what our approach is like, and on the other hand it begins to indicate what our methodology does reveal. Our aim is to understand how English comes to be 'produced' in the interaction of a multiplicity of (social) factors at work in the classroom. To do so, we need to connect issues of policy and social context, the characteristics and policies of urban multicultural schools, teacher formation and tradition, the ethos of English departments, and the political and institutional changes of the past decade with the issues of micro-level classroom interaction. All shape what English becomes in a specific site, and how it impacts on students' experiences of English and of learning English. However, the task of establishing a connection between this range of factors, and their actualization in multimodal form – the linking of macro-level social and policy factors and micro-level features, such as classroom practices of all kinds – is not at all straightforward.

A specific example of the kinds of question we have in mind here might be: 'How does a change, say, in policies around "selection" reflect itself, how does it "show up", in aspects of the English curriculum or in its pedagogy?' To establish the possibility of such a link we draw on semiotic theory and in particular on a social theory of 'sign'. Semiotics is the discipline that concerns itself with meaning of all kinds, in all forms, everywhere. Sign is the central concept of semiotics; it is an entity in which meaning and form have been brought together in a single unit – of signified and signifier, to use the technical terms – seen, always, as reflecting the meanings of those who make the sign. This relationship between social environment, signs, and the agency of those who make signs in the production of English are explored in all of the chapters that follow.

Policy is articulated in discourses of various kinds – of targets and attainment, of ability and achievement, of economic utility and cultural value. But it is only in their articulation as signs that discourses become 'visible' and effective. Signs are always multimodal and each modality brings the possibility of expressing and shaping meanings. A poster, part of a display on a wall for example, is a complex of signs: it may be a student's handwritten text, left with spelling and grammatical slips, rather than the word-processed writing of an official document, carefully edited, mounted on board rather than pinned up, laminated maybe, displayed in a prominent position or perhaps somewhere barely noticeable. When we look at such a poster-sign, the many meanings made as signs in the various modes are there in the one complex multimodal sign. The question is then how such complexes of meaning realize different aspects of the social life of the school, and that is discussed in many of the chapters following. In the example just given (a real instance from our data) each of the modal choices makes meaning and realizes a specific discourse among the many that are active in schools. For instance, how students' work is valued is lodged in a specific discourse around what it means to be a student; whether spontaneity counts more than careful work invested in editing is lodged in an educational discourse around learning, creativity, innovation, itself maybe part of a discourse around notions of human subjectivity. And the prominence given to student work may point to discursive contestation over the 'weight' to be given to students' agency relative to the demands of performativity, and so on.

Extract 2.2

From being an emergent and 'alternative' discourse associated with hippy culture in the 1970s, environmentalism has shifted to become a mainstream, dominant discourse in the twenty-first century. If English is to be a topical subject then it needs to be informed and responsive in relation to the discourse and debates of the environment. However, there is clearly no point in English teachers repeating the work of colleagues in geography and science who will be dealing with environment as subject content. Work in English needs an English flavour and is likely to focus on strategies of rhetoric and on how debates are represented in literature, non-fiction and media.

Care for the environment might seem to be an uncontroversial position but climate change – the most pressing issue – raises a number of controversial debates. Whereas climate change may be belatedly accepted as fact by all but a few climate change sceptics, the causes, the effects and particularly the solutions are vigorously contested according to differing political, moral and economic interests as well as different scientific theories. The complexity of the issue as a focus for debate can seem daunting and the scientific knowledge needed is often beyond the scope of English. One of the best ways to handle this is through collaboration with colleagues in geography and science. This collaboration can be in the planning, in joint teaching, or in raising the subject connections with pupils or through a mixture of all three approaches. It is also important to know if you are connecting with a topic that has already been covered in another subject area so that you can draw on and develop pupils' knowledge from a different perspective rather than going over well-trodden ground.

Many of the topics that are typically selected for debate in English could have a more explicit and informed environmental angle. For instance animal-related topics are commonly a focus for debate in English because children are powerfully and emotionally engaged by issues involving animals. Typical topics include zoos, vegetarianism, fox hunting, animal experiments and factory farming. These could all be related to environmental issues: for instance, zoos raise issues of species conservation and biodiversity; vegetarianism is not just a moral choice but also raises the issue of the strain on the world's ecosystems from reliance on meat; fox hunting could connect with issues of wildlife management; animal experiments could connect with the human manipulation of nature; and factory farming has detrimental impacts on the environment through hormone, pesticide and fertiliser use and the transmission of disease. The current focus of National Strategy-led teaching (DfEE 2001) in English lessons tends towards the encouragement of a rational rather than an emotional response, with pupils taught to distinguish between fact and opinion and to notice linguistic strategies for persuasion. Debates related to the environment are often part of a sequence of lessons on 'non-fiction', which will incorporate teaching objectives on persuasion in speech and writing for different audiences and discursive speech and writing. It is worth remembering the broader educational potential of these units of work. This chapter argues that the content and the values within these units *matter* and a topic such as climate change is not just a framework for teaching speaking and listening and literacy, although of course these are also important.

DfEE (2001) *Key Stage 3 National Strategy.* London: HMSO.

Extract 2.3

Towards the end of my first year of teaching in the English school system at an East London comprehensive school, I found myself faced with 800 of my students who had come out on strike. They had written some poems. I had published them locally and then been sacked because the authorities of the school had not liked them. The strike was the students' answer to having their work demeaned in this way. They demonstrated and sang in Stepney churchyard and on the waste ground outside the school gates in the pouring rain, brought other local schools out too in solidarity action, and marched from Stepney to Westminster, rallying again in Trafalgar Square and marching on to Downing Street in an attempt to bring their protest to the prime minister.

Those events proved to be a massive learning experience for me. I had been brought up to accept poetry and literature generally as a part of the English 'canon', sealed away from real life and its emotions; there to be read and studied as classical texts, but not lived and emulated, certainly not to be the cause of strikes and marches. 'Poetry makes nothing happen', W.H. Auden had written (and he was as modern a poet as had been admitted onto our university course); it only 'survives in the valley of its saying', but goes no further. The teenage poets of *Stepney Words* and their schoolmates had refused to accept that and had certainly made something happen, both for me and themselves. Through their action, support, and the publicity that it generated, I regained my job after a long legal battle. It was poetry that had provoked their cultural and collective action, with the strong support of parents, school cleaners and other local people, but primarily through their own intervention. These children of a multiracial working-class community had caused words to become actions.

I shall return to these events and their causes later in these pages, but for me as a teacher they had demonstrated upon my very pulses that the teaching and practice of language and poetry were anything but passive or detached pursuits, and when I went beyond the A level and university 'literature' curricula and read the writing of ordinary East Londoners that had emerged from the titanic struggles of labour over the previous century – the poetry and prose of dockers, matchgirls, tailors, gasworkers, Jews, Irish and Caribbean immigrants, Bangladeshis, Maltese and workers from China and Africa – I realized that there was another tradition of poetry allied to the lives and movement of working-class people that proved the antithesis of Auden's negative words. I sat for hours in the local history room of Mile End library reading the literature proudly published in the *Women's Dreadnaught*, in *Lansbury's Labour Weekly*, in the *East End News* and in the mass of trade union and strike journals and bulletins, in self-published or locally-published collections of poetry and fiction, that gave the heartbeat of the struggling communities not only of the past, but of the one which surrounded me beyond the library walls. I found a whole new literacy, a new curriculum of poetry and life embracing each other for the betterment of those whom it served, and I was determined to make this noble and purposeful use of language and the imagination the centre of any 'English' teaching in my classroom.

For here were words which truly reflected the world but just as truly were determined to transform it for the benefit of those who had the worst of it – whether in the close streets of East London or in the fields of India, the other cities of Europe, the villages of Africa or anywhere in the world where people struggled to better their lives. Words were there as their friends and allies, fused by an imaginative and cultural energy which caused them to combust into action. This sense of the explosive dynamism of language was reinforced in me during the two years that I worked as a secondary-school teacher in Mozambique (from 1976 to 1978). Newly free from Portuguese colonialism after a long armed struggle, the new nation and its liberators looked towards language and literacy as elements of the new armoury of change and development that would propel their new nation out of centuries of poverty, naked exploitation and imperial rule. One of its ministers (for almost all the Mozambique Liberation Front cadres wrote poems as a way of setting down their vision and hope) expressed the power of the people's language in these lines:

I will forge simple words
which even the children can understand

words which will enter every house
like the wind
and fall like red hot embers
on our people's souls.

In our land
Bullets are beginning to flower.

Jorge Rebelo

In the face of such experiences I could no longer see literacy or language itself as neutral or passive areas of learning. Neither could I uphold a pedagogy which stood outside of the struggle of downtrodden people, and allowed events both inside and outside of the classroom to take an unchallenged or unaltered course. Whether it was revolutionary Africa or East London, the direction of language teaching seemed to invoke the same imperative that language must be developed and used as an imaginative tool for the betterment of the lives of those who learned to use it, that the word served the world and those who struggled from below to make it theirs and their children's. Blessed were these word-makers, for together in language and action they would change and share the Earth.

Language and action: for my teaching the two became inseparable. Literacy was there to understand the world, then change it.

Extract 2.4

Is there, then, a very simple definition of multicultural literature? Is it just a way of referring to literature written by black authors? What, though, of the subject-matter of such literature? Is it also an element in the multicultural identity of *Young Warriors* that it tells a story of Maroon people? And what of the presence of the white Redcoat soldiers in the narrative? Does the fact that the novel enacts a conflict between organised groups of runaway Maroons and the colonial power make it more multicultural? To put it another way, would it have been a less multicultural text if Tommy and the other warriors had restricted themselves to hunting coneys?

Versions of multiculturalism had been given prominence in education even before my time at Oxford had begun. There is, in the Bullock Report, a recognition of the relevance of students' out-of-school identities and experiences to what happens in the classroom:

No child should be expected to cast off the language and culture of the home as he crosses the school threshold, nor to live and act as though school and home represent two totally separate and different cultures which have to be kept firmly apart. (DES 1975, 286)

Such pluralist notions were always contested. Barely a year after the publication of the Bullock Report, the speech that James Callaghan, the then Prime Minister, made at Ruskin College, signalled an agenda for education that has continued to dominate the discourse of policy throughout the intervening three decades: the focus on basic skills, on standards and reductive versions of accountability has left little space for more nuanced considerations of curriculum and pedagogy. Shortly after I had started work in Tower Hamlets, the Bullock Report's commitment to more locally accountable, student- and community-centred approaches was effaced in official discourse by an entirely different model of the relation between students' lives and identities outside school, on the one hand, and, on the other, the school curriculum. When the consultation paper on the National Curriculum was published (DES 1987), it used the language of progressivism, the language of difference, in a statement of entitlement that denied any curricular space for the exploration of difference, of subjectivity. This was, quite explicitly, to be a one–size–fits–all curriculum, one that ensured

> that all pupils, regardless of sex, ethnic origin and geographical location, have access to broadly the same good and relevant curriculum and programmes of study. (DES 1987, 4)

In this paradigm, the school curriculum, detailed in the programmes of study, derives its validity not from its responsiveness to local interests but from its universality. And, if the curriculum is to be 'broadly the same', little space is left for any serious attention to be paid to what Bullock termed 'the language and culture of the home'. The key word here is 'regardless': local differences – of gender, history, culture – are to be disregarded. Equality of opportunity is to be delivered through access to a homogeneous, preformed entity, the already-specified curriculum. One might be permitted to wonder about the meaning of 'relevant' in this context. Relevant to what, or to whom? What does such relevance look like? This formulation has, nonetheless, been massively influential. If one enters 'curriculum' and 'regardless' as link terms in an Internet search engine such as Google, one finds hundreds of UK school websites, all of them proclaiming their commitment to providing a curriculum that is beneficial precisely because it is delivered 'regardless' of the identities and specific characteristics of its students.

Perhaps part of the reason for this universalist curriculum promise/ premise is that it distances schooling from the dangerously controversial territory of identity politics while simultaneously colonising the language of equality of opportunity. What could be more egalitarian than a commitment to a common curriculum? And what, at the same time, could be more comforting to those who fear social fragmentation and who regard the curriculum as a means of both asserting and reestablishing a single, national identity?

It is instructive to contrast this notion of universality with the other strand of official discourse on the relation between students and the curriculum. If pre-existent, social aspects of the students are to be discounted, individual psychological traits are important determiners of appropriate curricula. Schools may even choose students on the basis of a perceived aptitude (for music, for languages, or whatever). And it has been a consistent feature of government thinking about the curriculum that the choices that students make about courses should be based on a sense of their individual strengths, interests and aptitudes. The foundation for the current mania for specialist schools is thus some rather fanciful notion that children, or their parents, should at the age of 11 opt for a school that specialises in languages (or media arts, or 'business and enterprise') because they have already discerned a particular aptitude for these pursuits.

The centralised model of the curriculum, promoted by the 1987 consultation document and by the earlier HMI *Curriculum Matters* publications (DES 1984), continues to underpin the most recent policy pronouncements around the theme of 'personalisation', to the extent that personalisation has been carefully defined as a set of increasingly individualised interventions to ensure access to the same pre-specified curricular goals. Here is Ken Boston, the head of the Qualifications and Curriculum Authority, speaking at the launch of the latest version of the National Curriculum:

We now know that to maximise the learning for each individual, we must first measure the level of progress that the student has reached (which is called 'assessment for learning'); we must then plan and deliver the learning necessary to enable the pupil to advance to the next level of progress (which is called 'personalised learning').

The development of such a customised or child-centred approach to teaching and learning is not some new-age obsession with making students feel good, or any rejection of the importance of formal teaching, or a drift from discipline-based curriculum: it is the internationally proven research-based strategy for improving learning and raising attainment at individual, school and national level. (Boston 2007)

Implicit in the 1987 consultation document's notion of 'access' is a particular pedagogy, one that was rendered more explicit in the increasingly frequent appearance of the phrase 'pupils should be taught to . . .' in subsequent versions of the National Curriculum (DES/Welsh Office 1990; DfE/Welsh Office 1995; DfEE 1999). The assumption is that what is learnt is equivalent to what is taught, that knowledge can be transmitted, and that, in effect, a curriculum can be delivered (like a sack of coal, or potatoes). Ken Boston's view of personalised learning emphasises important elements of continuity with what has gone before. Learning remains, in his presentation, linear, measurable and the property of the individual learner. His version of teaching might be more fine-grained than the versions on which earlier incarnations of the National Curriculum were premised; it is, nonetheless, a deeply technicist approach to pedagogy.

Moreover, when Boston is at pains to define what his (official) version of personalisation is *not*, it seems to me that all the strands that he caricatures and then rejects are aspects of practice that need to be taken seriously. I might not be committed to a 'new-age obsession with making students feel good', but I worry about approaches to teaching and learning that fail to take sufficient account of the subjectivities of the learner, that fail, therefore, to conceptualise teaching and learning as relational, socioculturally situated practices. Likewise, though I am not sure exactly what Boston means by the 'rejection of the importance of formal teaching', I want to explore approaches to pedagogy that are more conscious of the agency of the learners. And if Boston wants to allay fears that what is on offer is a 'drift from discipline-based curriculum', I want to suggest that there is a pressing need to look closely (and critically) at the ways in which the current discipline-based curriculum is negotiated and realised in the urban classroom.

Part of what seems to me deeply problematic about curriculum policy post-Bullock is that it does not reflect my experience in the (multicultural, urban) classroom. What attracted me, more than 20 years ago, to Bullock's advice that students should not be 'expected to cast off the language and culture of the home' was that it gestured at a more inclusive, pluralist

77

conception of schooling. In other words, my initial reaction was an ideological one, supportive of what appeared to me to be a move in the direction of a more socially just education system. What I did not appreciate then, I think, was the force of Bullock's words in relation to pedagogy: students do not – *cannot* – simply cast off their out-of-school identities and histories as they enter the classroom. The question is, therefore, what opportunities there are for them to deploy these cultural resources in their learning within the classroom. The danger of that one word, 'regardless' is that it encourages an approach to curriculum and pedagogy that is inattentive to such cultural resources.

Boston, K. (2007) *Speech at the launch of the National Curriculum*. London: QCA.

DES (1975) *A Language for Life*. London: HMSO.

DES (1987) *The National Curriculum 5–16: A Consultation Document*. London: HMSO.

DES (1984) *Curriculum Matters*. London: HMSO.

DES/Welsh Office (1990) *English in the National Curriculum*. London: HMSO.

DfE/Welsh Office (1995) *English in the National Curriculum*. London: HMSO.

DfEE (1999) *The National Curriculum*. London: HMSO.

Exploratory questions

- How significant is multi-modality in the contemporary English classroom? What place, if any, remains for 'literature'?
- How far should English teachers concern themselves with multi-cultural issues as represented in texts, given that the subject's name remains, for better or worse, 'English'?
- Searle outlines professional experiences from some years ago: his, and his pupils', struggle for recognition of their lived experiences and how these relate to language and texts; how far, in your view, have matters changed (progressed?) since then?
- Matthewman's eco-critical approach to texts deserves serious attention; in your experience, how likely is it that English teachers will change or develop their practice in view of her persuasive arguments? Will you?

Further reading

I have tried here to present a range of material concerning the place of texts in English pedagogy, from diverse perspectives. Neil Astley's Bloodaxe Books has been instrumental in enlivening poetry for young people through several anthologies, including this one; the Introduction is well worth reading in its own right as a passionate defence of poetry's place in contemporary culture. Sue Dymoke too looks carefully at poetry teaching in secondary English, especially the much-neglected area of teaching its writing, while Marjorie Hourd's 1949 book gives a carefully reasoned and exemplified account of the positive nature of poetry teaching. Jill Pirrie's *On Common Ground* relates her experiences as an English teacher in Suffolk, enthusiastically – and expertly – inspiring her young pupils to write some excellent poems, several of which won major poetry writing competitions. Sasha Matthewman's paper gives vivid illustration of the pedagogical possibilities for teaching a particular poem along eco-critical lines, as discussed above.

John Berger's classic text, mingling illustration with words, aims to do exactly what's implied by the title: foster stimulating ways of seeing the world. In this, Berger prefigures media and multi-modal textual interests, as described in David Buckingham and Julian Sefton-Green's succinct paper. Gabrielle Cliff Hodges et al. present narrative, in multiple forms, as the mainstay of English, and Jackie Marsh and Elaine Millard suggest ways of drawing on that greatest resource for all English teachers: the pupils themselves. John Dollimore and Alan Sinfield consider Shakespeare teaching in radical context: a book well worth reading alongside Rex Gibson's *Teaching Shakespeare*. Finally, Louise Rosenblatt's seminal work explores the nature of reading, drawing especially from reader-response theory.

Astley, N. (2002) Introduction, in N. Astley (ed.) *Staying Alive: Real Poems for Unreal Times*. Tarset: Bloodaxe Books.

Berger, J. (1972) *Ways of Seeing*. Harmondsworth: Penguin.

Buckingham, D. and Sefton-Green, J. (1994) Making Sense of the Media: From Reading to Culture, in S. Brindley (ed.) *Teaching English*. London: Routledge.

Cliff Hodges, G., Drummond, M.J. and Styles, M. (eds) (2000) *Tales, Tellers and Texts*. London: Cassell.

Dollimore, J. and Sinfield, A. (1985) *Political Shakespeare*. Manchester: Manchester University Press.

Dymoke, S. (2003) *Drafting and Assessing Poetry*. London: Paul Chapman.

Hourd, M. (1949) *The Education of the Poetic Spirit*. London: Heinemann.

Marsh, J. and Millard, E. (2000) *Literacy and Popular Culture: Using Children's Culture in the Classroom*. London: Paul Chapman.

Matthewman, S. (2007) But what about the fish? Teaching Ted Hughes' *Pike* with Environmental Bite, *English in Education* 41.3, 67–77.

Pirrie, J. (1987) *On Common Ground*. London: Hodder & Stoughton.

Rosenblatt, L. (1995) *Literature as Exploration*. New York: The Modern Language Association of America.

5

The arts context for secondary English

There has long been in the forefront of English pedagogical theory and practice an influential tendency – perhaps *the* influential tendency – envisaging the subject as essentially located in an arts paradigm. Within this broad church, including several important commentators from outside mainstream English, many write and practise within an effectively Romantic tradition in English pedagogy, including such notable commentators as Sampson, Holbrook, Rosen and Knight (albeit in their very different ways): a tradition that could be helpfully characterized as combining the most creative, non-instrumental aspects of English teaching and learning (sometimes rather clumsily grouped together under the umbrella titles of 'cultural heritage' and 'personal expression'). To do many of these writers full justice, however, we need also to credit them with a powerful critical edge: to use terms more likely to be encountered in exponents of critical pedagogy, following Paulo Freire, for at their most lucid they combine elements of a 'language of critique' with a 'language of possibility'.

Part 1: English pedagogy in the broad contexts of creativity and the arts

Sources

1.1 Abbs, P. (2003) *Against the Flow: Education, the Arts and Postmodern Culture.* London: RoutledgeFalmer.
1.2 Stevens, D. and McGuinn, N. (2004) *The Art of Teaching Secondary English.* London: RoutledgeFalmer.

1.3 Harrison, B. (1983) *English Studies 11–18: An Arts-based Approach*. London: Hodder & Stoughton.

Introduction

The three excerpts here deal with the background of creativity insofar as it informs the theory and practice of English teaching and learning. Peter Abbs, whose work we have already met in similar contexts, and Bernard Harrison each appeals especially to the Romantic tradition of self-expression through the arts, often focusing on the nature of the imagination, as do I in my own writing. However, as suggested above, there is a danger of over-simplifying often complex and sophisticated arguments, and each of the writers has particular things to say about the nature of the creativity espoused and its relationship to other facets of English, such as critical literacy, values in the curriculum, and the practicalities of the classroom.

Extract 1.1

My aim is to delineate and evoke three aspects of understanding and affirmation, three modes of cognitive apprehension that carry with them elements of the numinous and the transcendent. I would, also, like to state at the outset that while I believe literature and the arts serve many purposes – historical, ideological, linguistic, psychological – their quintessential value relates to what I can only call life-understanding, life-enhancement, life-wisdom. The arts, at their best, deepen and refine our sense of what it means to be alive; they open out existential possibilities for our lives; they invite us to see again free of the grimy occluding stains of habit, free from the easy smears and cheap distortions of received opinion. At times they disturb, even terrify, but they do so in order to liberate, in order to give birth to some kind of insight, some kind of wisdom. This is a most unfashionable view, a view against the flow, but it seems to me, nonetheless, *true*. After all, today's most fierce fashions are nearly always tomorrow's most facile deceptions.

It is my working assumption throughout this book that the arts matter because they serve – at their best – the deep human impulse to understand, to integrate and to transcend; they serve life's ineradicable desire to live more fully, more abundantly. I have always felt that art and, especially, the making of art enables individuals to ratchet up their ephemeral lives to the level of high symbolic adventure and philosophical questing.

[. . .]

What, then, are the three faces of wisdom?

The first face I will call the epiphanic. This will refer to the poem – or the painting or work of art – which sings out of affirmation, the moment of mesmerized revelation. It tends to utter its appreciation in the present tense and would have us, as readers or listeners, catch the beauty and incandescence of the thing seen or, rather, witnessed. It is invariably rhapsodic in character and marks a moment of fusion where the quotidian divisions of subject and object are transcended. My main exemplar here will be James Joyce.

The second face, in contrast, is the Socratic. This is the deeply questioning, the frowning face of wisdom. The Socratic is analytical and takes nothing for granted. It strips away the habitual protections provided by collective opinion or cosy subjectivity. It can appear profoundly negative, even destructive, and yet, I will argue, it is one essential means for keeping the mind on high alert, for keeping the truth open, for preventing the descent of original insight or creative perplexity into reductive platitudes and the daily junk mail of clichés. Here I will take the American poet, Emily Dickinson, as my exemplar.

The third face is the prophetic. If the epiphanic and the Socratic tend to work out of the present tense, the prophetic depends on the conjectural power of the future tense and the subjunctive. It presupposes a power to apprehend possibilities not in the immediate push and press of immediate exigencies, but in the future, tomorrow, next year, in a thousand years time, even at the end of time as, conceivably, the universe contracts to its original state. This leap into time future, enhanced enormously by the buttressing grammar of language and tiny conjectural phrases like 'what if', gives us the power of prophecy, of envisaging other universes, of offering hope and desolation, of utopia and dystopia, of distant galaxies and ultimate dust. My main example here will be the poet and engraver, William Blake.

Extract 1.2

I would argue that imagination is the means of finding value and, as such, is implicit in all educative processes; its particular significance for English is in the study of the ways in which value and values are embedded in language itself.

Relevant, too, is the idea of originality, although care is needed here to avoid any celebration of originality simply for its own sake, or any inevitably frustrated insistence on total originality – which clearly would be well nigh impossible to achieve except at some cutting edge activity in any given discipline. In a way, of course, everything is original, in that the precise circumstances and conditions are unique to the occurrence; in another way, nothing is – for we must always work with whatever resources and ideas already exist. The English classroom should acknowledge both these apparently contradictory senses of originality – celebrating the moments of creativity on the one hand, and working within the discipline of study on the other. The emphasis in the context of *All Our Futures* is on individual originality ('a person's work may be original in relation to their own previous work and output') or on relative originality ('original in relation to their peer group; to other young people of the same age, for example'), and it would not be hard to find excellent examples of both in our schools – although actual recognition of what we find might be rather more of a challenge, and perhaps would be more unusual.

In classroom practice, it is the dynamic relationship between the previously cited four elements (using imagination, pursuing purposes, being original, judging value), and the skills needed to realise them, that gives rise to meaningful creativity. And yet the subject English itself is not always seen or constructed primarily as a 'creative' discipline – indeed, the current emphasis on functional literacy may be seen as something of an erosion of notions of creativity in the classroom.

[. . .]

. . . All this rather begs some important questions concerning the meaning and validity of creativity, and why it is especially valuable. If, indeed, it is valuable, then a sense of value lies at its heart. As has been suggested previously, in discussions about instrumental rationality and its implications, it is possible to act creatively, as is commonly understood by the term, for highly questionable ends: exploitative, destructive, damaging. To make radical social meaning in the context of teaching and learning, creativity needs to be situated in a coherent place of values. Creativity's minute particularities, its celebratory subjectivities, its potential for social meaning-making, its liberating connective power only really come to life when values are emphasised.

But what and whose values? As so often, the answer lies in the framing of the question: in the sense that values are culturally specific and, as such, are contested – often energetically, sometimes creatively, and sometimes destructively. There are, indeed, multiple places for creativity, and each relates to the cultural context. In a way, this implies multiculturalism, but I am, here, more interested in the connections between places, and by this route between creativity and value. With the stress on connections – relationships, contrasts, compatibilities – it may be more helpful to suggest an intercultural rather than merely a multicultural understanding of creativity and value. The implication of this kind of understanding is that creativity may be placed in multiple sites and have roots in diverse cultural values, and that it is in the relationships between these entities – the 'inter' of the intercultural project – that deep value-laden meaning may be both found and made. Importantly, this conception is suggestive of both individual and social transformation, as the damaging distinction between the two is eroded.

[. . .]

At the centre of concern here is what Brecht aptly called 'Lebenskunst', the creative art of life itself. If intercultural variety and vitality are the aims, they must also be the means – and the culture of the classroom is that which both stimulates and emanates from the totality of experience. That familiar unit of school-based time, the lesson – with all its generally ignored spiritual connotations fully acknowledged here – must, in some sense or other, become a microcosm of broader issues. I have in mind here, particularly, a Romantic transformative model, through which innocence is brought into some sort of relationship – even one based on conflict – with experience. In a fully dialectical process, fostered by careful teaching, the interplay between innocence as thesis and experience as antithesis may lead to a higher, fuller awareness – based on innocence in the Blakean sense of wonder, but acknowledging and encompassing the nature of, often harsh, experience. This culmination may be conceptualised as a kind of synthesis which, of course, will then play its part in further dialectical encounters. For the Romantics – Blake perhaps especially – this sort of transformative model provided insights into the development of the human psyche, individually, historically and socially. In the same way as each individual struggles in his or her life with this fundamental transformative process in a fully social context, so too must human institutions and the various elements that comprise them. School itself is one of the most basic of those institutions, but I am more interested here in smaller, more manageable units within school: the lesson, particularly, and the classroom.

Extract 1.3

The main roots of a language are nourished through artistic activity. Art is the revealing of the human quest for truth. And that, let it be added, is the goal of all creative discourse, and of all authentic learning. It is what we are about, at best, in using, teaching and learning language.

It follows, that as teachers of language we should recognise the primary importance for our lives of all the expressive arts – kinetic, visual, musical, literary, verbal. As learners or teachers, we seek then to be continually engaged and re-engaged in art disciplines – especially, of course, in the language arts of literature, drama, art-speech. These are the disciplines through which English studies will flourish, and which offer, at best, a true basis for any genuinely individual expression of experience . . . The nature of art-discourse, in any kind of language context, lies in its being an authentic expression of questing thought by you and me, when every word, phrase and pause counts in revealing the witness of the living individual and its impact on the listener and reader. There should always be art-discourse; or (to modify just a little) the roots of art-speech should always be nourishing the discourse of the learner, the teacher, the living human being. It is indeed the teacher's responsibility to allow – and even, when necessary, coerce – the learner to acknowledge and take up full responsibility for and commitment to what he says. But the 'coercing' must be of that rare kind which simply insists on respect for the self-being of the learner, and which is prepared to wait for the learner's self-responsibility to emerge. For the learner's own language is redolent of his/her otherness – it is of his/her body. Discovering the world through touch, vision, hearing, smelling, tasting, and giving shapes to these discoveries in language forms: these are acts of the body, through which personal meanings are offered and shared. The individual's experience comes in turn to affect the public meanings that we hold in common, within our several contexts.

[. . .]

The source of such notions goes back at least to the beginnings of the Romantic Movement. It springs specifically from Wordsworth's treatise on poetry and language, in *The Preface* to the *Lyrical Ballads*, a text which has found its way into virtually every important discussion about the language of poetry ever since. In the *Preface*, Wordsworth advances his central point about the nature of poetry – that 'there neither is nor can be any essential difference' between poetry and prose, for they 'both speak by and to the same organs'. And in itself, the *Preface* provides its own evidence as to the nature of art-discourse, whether as prose or poetry. It stands as a heartfelt personal statement about the nature of language and poetry, and is at the same time a classic piece of strenuously argued rational discourse. Reason serves emotion, emotion employs reason, as the writer works sincerely at the effort to say what he means, from what he has felt. The writer is an ordinary man, who is also a poet 'speaking to men.

[. . .]

Thus entrusted and encouraged, thus engaged and quickened, learners may then seek to shape their own language patterns, to make sure of their living according to their own variant individuality. For our very being is lodged in our language, as our language is in our being; and only through our language can we declare ourselves to others, to the world, thus validating both ourselves and the world.

Yet how much English teaching and language 'intervention' is genuinely composed of serious play in the spirit of these truths, is a respectful negotiating between teacher and learners of their several experiences – of text, or film, or event, or moral issue? . . . But if we intend to work from real 'basics', we cannot forget one quite basic truth about the acquiring of language: that living language is interwoven with living being. Thus to intervene in, or even simply to encourage language development is potentially to enter private, even secret areas. Respect for the otherness of the learner is of the essence. We find the notion of physical 'cloning' repugnant; why should we then be any more patient with language-learning 'programmes' which assume a right to predict an undeviating path of language development for an individual?

Exploratory questions

- All three extracts make significant claims for the arts as the basis of education, and specifically the subject English; in your practical experience, are these claims justified?
- What may be the practical implications of creativity as the basis of the subject English in terms of day-to-day classroom teaching and learning?
- Does the location of English as primarily an arts subject imply certain limitations with regard to other possible aspects of the subject, both theoretically and practically?
- For the Abbs extract, do you find the 'three faces of wisdom' – the epiphanic, Socratic, and prophetic, as outlined in the extract – helpful as guides for the practice of English teaching?
- Poetry especially, and literature more generally, tend to be singled out as central to an arts-based vision of English; can this be justified, given the multiplicity of other texts, often more readily available in everyday life, that influence our (and our pupils') lives?

Part 2: English, drama and the visual arts

Sources

2.1 Fleming, M. (2010) *English Teaching in the Secondary School*, Ch. 9 Drama. London: Routledge.

2.2 Heathcote, D. (1967) Improvisation, *English in Education* 1.3; reprinted in J. N. Britton (ed.) (1984) *Teaching English: An International Exchange*. London: Heinemann.

2.3 Benton, M. (2000) *Studies in the Spectator Role: Literature, Painting and Pedagogy*. London: RoutledgeFalmer.

Introduction

Dorothy Heathcote's pioneering work on drama in education has had – and continues to have – immense impact on that subject's practice in schools and beyond. It has also had great influence on English teaching, whether through collaboration with drama departments, or as integrated into the specifically English curriculum. Rex Gibson's work on 'active Shakespeare', for example (see Chapter 4), has drawn significantly on her work. Mike Fleming too has done much to influence the teaching of drama and English, seeking to synthesize various traditions and show how all parts of the secondary curriculum may benefit from dramatic approaches.

Michael Benton, on the other hand, has developed visual literacy as fundamental to English pedagogy in an arts-based context, in this respect building imaginatively on the work of James Britton. In this he, and his brother Peter Benton, with whom he has frequently collaborated, has much in common with many others – including those with a more media-based interest in visual literacy, and has developed the work of John Berger and others (see Chapter 4).

Extract 2.1

In much of the contemporary literature on drama teaching there are often few grounds for discriminating between one sort of practice and another. At one time this was provided by a distinction between 'drama' (with its emphasis on engagement and quality of experience) and 'theatre' (with its emphasis on acting and performance) but, as suggested above, those divisions are simply not tenable. With the increased publication of lesson schemes on websites and from bodies such as the QCA it is useful to have some criteria for discriminating between one sort of practice and another.

The three concepts 'dramatic play', 'drama as art' and 'role-play/simulation' provide a helpful means of making a critical distinction between drama practices and understanding why drama teaching can be difficult. Drama has its origins in the dramatic play of young children – that is part of its appeal. Pupils are always liable to revert to having fun and playing in their drama, much to the frustration of teachers who are looking for serious commitment: the shipwreck culminates in a hilarious fight with sharks; the bank robbery descends into a chaotic shooting battle; the confrontation between friends ends in an unconvincing fist fight. This sort of reaction is often misinterpreted as bad behaviour. Sometimes it is, but more often it arises because the pupils do not know what else to do. This type of pupil reaction, which is not uncommon because it is 'natural', is not acknowledged often enough in the books on drama.

There is another type of practice in drama which could be termed 'role-play or simulation'. There is nothing wrong with role-play and many teachers who have witnessed pupils engage in the kind of dramatic playing described above would be delighted if pupils settled down to engage in some role-play in the classroom. As with all language and concepts there is no clear-cut distinction here – simple definitions are not helpful. However, role-play tends to be simple and two-dimensional (as opposed to drama as art, which has more depth). It involves the surface imitation of real-life situations such as a client asking for a loan from a bank manager. It is a very useful device in teaching – hence the title of this section 'recognising drama at its best' not 'recognising good drama'. The term 'simulation' is being used here to refer to activities which require participants to 'go through the motions' without any sense of complexity or depth. Thus a meeting in a town hall discussing a new bypass can be set up by giving pupils role cards: 'you are the shopkeeper and you object to the bypass because it will take business away'.

In contrast 'drama as art' seeks to weave in a greater level of depth and nuances of meaning. Suppose the client and bank manager knew each other when they were younger and one used to bully the other or stole his girlfriend – the acting now has a hidden dimension. The shopkeeper arguing against the bypass does not want to appear selfish so his argument is actually based on children's safety – although others in the meeting are suspicious of his real motives. Drama as art looks for 'multi-levels' and subtexts whereas role-play and simulation tends to operate on surface levels of meaning. A tableau can operate as a form of simulation ('create a wedding photograph') or can tend more towards drama ('create a wedding photograph which shows a truth about the relationships', e.g. the best man and bride were former lovers).

The point here is not to create a sense of drama as something rarefied and elitist. This happened far too often in the 1970s and 1980s when demonstration drama lessons which were intensely moving were very hard to recreate in the classroom. Writing about drama should not make the subject too remote nor should its challenges be unacknowledged. The teaching point is that pupils can often find role-play and simulation activities dull, and they can become lacking in motivation. Dramatic playing can be superficially fun but in the end unrewarding. When evaluating suggestions for drama lessons it is a good idea to avoid recommendations which are likely to lead pupils too readily towards dramatic playing, such as when they are told to get into groups and act something out without sufficient support, focus and direction. It is also wise to avoid lessons which are unlikely to engage pupils' interest because they operate too mechanically and too much on the surface.

Extract 2.2

Improvisation in my view means 'discovering by trial, error and testing; using available materials with respect for their nature, and being guided by this appreciation of their potential'. The *end-product* of improvisation is the *experience* of it. Any artist in any field will tell you this. What, then, is improvisation in drama? Kenneth Tynan's definition of drama will help here. In *Declaration* he states, 'Good Drama for me is made up of the thoughts, the words and the gestures that are wrung from human beings, on their way to, or in, or emerging from, a state of desperation'. Obviously, then, dramatic improvisation is concerned with what we discover for ourselves and the group when we place ourselves in a human situation containing some element of desperation. Very simply it means putting yourself into other people's shoes and, by using personal experience to help you to understand their point of view, you may discover more than you knew when you started. What this 'more' is depends upon the purpose of the exercise in the first place, i.e. what the motivation was. More of this later.

We use this system of discovery, naturally, all the time – it seems inborn in us, as natural as breathing – in our first playing, in our reading for pleasure where we share the lives of others, thus stretching our experience; when we seek to understand another person as in friendship and caring; in the world offered by cinema, TV, radio and the theatre. This of course is always a *personal* role-playing, *personally* motivated, whereas the class is a group which requires motivating at specified times during the school day. The mystery has arisen partly because of this, and because the real issues have been clouded by theatre and 'showing' issues, both laudable in themselves and to be desired in their place.

It can now be seen, I hope, that improvisation is not a subject area (though it *may* be so sometimes), it is really a tool for the teacher, to be used flexibly at times when 'personal identity' role-playing is the most efficient way of crystallizing what the teacher wishes to make clear. It is available to teachers of science as well as of the arts, though it will *possibly* be employed by the former in a somewhat more limited form. 'Possibly' – because we have not yet done sufficient research into matters like this, but wherever understanding of human behaviour, feelings, hopes and attitudes is required it will function speedily and efficiently. It must be understood at this stage that I am not writing of the improvisation used by children in their own play, or of the improvisation used in class when the teacher takes up the position of onlooker in order to enable children to have child-drama opportunities. I am concerned, here, solely with the use of improvisation to aid a learning/teaching situation, and many child-drama elements will be present in a well-conducted one – it cannot really succeed if they are not. An example used recently with a fourth form in a secondary school will serve to illustrate what I mean. The main purpose of the work was to try to break down the verbal shyness of the form (remember this all the time as you read on!). So the teacher began with the question, 'If we had a million pounds to spend for the good of humanity, on what would we spend it?' The debate ranged over Oxfam, 'the pill' for India, research into cultivation of deserts, Cheshire Homes, geriatric and maternity wards, and for a time remained polite and uninspired. But as soon as the class were asked to explain Oxfam and, in this case, the use of a modern highly efficient plough, to the teacher, who became an Indian peasant anxious only to work the land of his ancestors in the way his father before him had done, then the real and deeper issues were thrown in their faces. Once the deep issues were raised, the class worked in a different dimension of communication and no longer could it remain at a polite level, it became a series of personal committals, highly demanding and equally satisfying. This class of children were astonished at their ability to become involved in the problems of an Indian farmer and even more astonished at their ability to *express* their involvement. Because the teacher's aim was to help the children to enjoy verbal communication via argument, role-playing, debate and discussion, he did not allow the situation to be developed as a *play*; he kept the verbal challenge as the first priority.

Extract 2.3

The comparative study of the verbal and visual arts is dangerous territory. Its allure is self-evident both in the long, intertwined history of the sister arts of poetry and painting and in the burgeoning critical commentary it has attracted, particularly in the last two decades. In the professional litera-ture, warnings proliferate about the pitfalls in attempting to theorise two art forms that, whatever their links, remain distinct. The main principle of this cautionary tale was set out by Hagstrum who, drawing on classical precedents, argued that 'Each of the mimetic arts achieves its proper pleasure in its proper medium' and that 'Each must take into perpetual account its own peculiar limitations' (Hagstrum 1958: 6). Subsequently, Wark has elaborated upon this position, stressing the differences between literary criticism and art history. In addition to the issue of authenticity, which is fundamental to art history in a way that is not true for literature, Wark also discusses several related matters to which attention has been drawn in previous chapters. While acknowledging that visual art has gained much from the work of literary critics, he offers some cautions about inter-disciplinary studies. In particular, art historians are concerned with a knowledge of medium and technique, with how the visual artefact came into being through, say, sketch book drawings, or preliminary studies. Typically, they rely on external evidence to corroborate an interpretation of a work of art more than literary critics do who, in turn, are readier to interpret from the simple evidence before their eyes. The student of litera-ture may tend to look at paintings more for their subject-matter than for their form or style, a tension that is present when we speak of reading, as opposed to viewing, paintings (Wark 1983: 26–35). The distinctive qualities of word and image should be constant reminders. 'The image begins where the word vanishes. The word begins where the image vanishes.' Edna Longley stresses the essential difference between the arts – the 'separation of artistic powers after the mysterious point of imaginative origin'. She urges us to 'explore relationship-in-difference . . . rather than try to homogenise' (Longley 1994: 228–9).

I have tried to be alert to these dangers in exploring the notion of spectatorship across the two arts. Part I of this book was at pains to celebrate difference as well as to note similarity. Spectatorship was presented as the central concept in aesthetic response to literature and painting. The discussions in Part II suggest that this concept can be 'unpacked' into the experiences of looking, seeing and perceiving. The issues that each raises are ones I have considered before in respect of paintings (Benton 1992: 108) and which now I wish to extend to literature. In *looking*, the focus is upon what happens *to* the eye; in *seeing*, the focus is upon what happens *behind* the eye; and, in *perceiving*, the focus is upon what happens *beyond* the eye. Looking concerns matters of reader or viewer reception – what the eye and brain do as they travel back and forth along lines of print, or range over a picture on a canvas. Looking answers the 'What?' question of aesthetic response; it affirms what is the object of contemplation and the artistic status that we give it. Seeing concerns matters of conception – the sense we develop of the means by which the work has created its effects; and that increasing awareness of how parts do, or (from a postmodernist perspective) do not, relate to the whole. Seeing answers the 'How?' question and involves us in acknowledging the poem or painting as a verbal or visual construct. Perceiving concerns the making of meaning – the ways in which an interpretation of an art work is formed; it takes us beyond the immediacy of the aesthetic moment and draws upon our intertextual knowledge and our awareness of the personal and cultural conditions in which the poem or painting had been created. Perceiving answers the 'Why?' question and may take us some way towards discovering why the artist wrote or painted a particular work.

Such formulations have a beguiling neatness. Clearly, they are not discrete phases that spectators experience in linear fashion over the period of time that they are reading or viewing. There is overlapping and merging as spectators engage/disengage, or become engrossed in or detached from the art work. Understanding a poem or painting may come instantaneously as a flash of insight, or slowly build up as we (re)read or (re)view. Making meanings in the two arts is an unpredictable, idiosyncratic process affected by a host of variables in the context, culture and experience of the reader or viewer. Looking, seeing and perceiving are, perhaps, best seen as subsets of spectatorship, as types of activity that recur and enable us to make fuller and more satisfying readings of the literary and visual texts that we encounter.

Benton, M. (1992) *Secondary Worlds*. Milton Keynes: Open University Press.

Hagstrum J. (1958) *The Sister Arts*. Chicago, IL: Chicago University Press.

Longley, E. (1994) 'No more poems about paintings' in *The Living Steam*. Newcastle-upon-Tyne: Bloodaxe.

Wark, R. (1983) The weak sister's view of the sister arts, in Wendorf, R. (ed.) *Articulate Image*. Minneapolis, MI: Minnesota University Press.

Exploratory questions

- How close should the relationship be, ideally, between drama and English, given that drama departments, in practice, often seek to safeguard their independence?
- Within English, in your own professional practice, do you find drama approaches especially useful? If so, in what contexts?
- Drama has never been designated a separate subject in National Curriculum terms; the drama that is officially represented is subsumed under the English orders. Do you feel this is a limitation or advantage?
- How important is visual literacy to you as an English teacher? In terms of multi-modality, touched on in previous chapters, is its influence gaining ground?
- How may visual literacy fit into a specifically arts-based vision of English?

Further reading

Mike Fleming, Jonathan Neelands and Andy Kempe have all written helpful books on the nature of drama teaching and how such approaches may be used to positive effect in English contexts: a sample of their work is listed here, as well as a useful collection of Dorothy Heathcote's writing (Johnson and O'Neill). Herbert Read's subtle polemic, now a classic in all senses, is well worth reading as a defence of arts education, which he sees as basic to all creative teaching and learning. Read's influence has been profound and wide-ranging, including on such commentators as the Bentons, seeking to integrate poetry and painting in a practical classroom-based context. From a slightly different perspective, Elliott Eisner, an American arts educator, writes lucidly about the nature of the arts curriculum and its theoretical dimension; his influence on English teaching is growing, and is acknowledged positively by practitioners such as Bethan Marshall.

Benton, M. and Benton, P. (1990) *Double Vision*. London: Hodder & Stoughton.

Benton, M. and Benton, P. (1995) *Painting with Words*. London: Hodder & Stoughton.

Benton, M. and Benton, P. (1997) *Picture Poems*. London: Hodder & Stoughton.

Eisner, E. (2002) *The Arts and the Creation of Mind*. New Haven, CT: Yale University Press.

Fleming, M. (1997) *The Art of Drama Teaching*. London: David Fulton.

Fleming, M. (2003) *Starting Drama Teaching*. London: David Fulton.

Johnson, L. and O'Neill, C. (1984) *Dorothy Heathcote: Collected Writings on Education and Drama*. London: Hutchinson.

Kempe, A. and Nicholson, H. (2007) *Learning to Teach Drama 11–18*. London: Continuum.

Marshall, B. (2001) Creating Danger: The Place of the Arts in Education Policy, in A. Craft, B. Jeffrey and M. Leibling (eds) *Creativity in Education*. London: Continuum.

National Advisory Committee on Creative and Cultural Education (NACCCE) (1999) *All Our Futures: Creativity, Culture and Education*. London: DfEE.

Neelands, J. (1990) *Structuring Drama Work*. Cambridge: Cambridge University Press.

Read, H. (1958) *Education through Art*. London: Faber & Faber.

6 Assessment and evaluation issues

Assessment and the subject English – at least as conceived of by many commentators, several of whom are represented in these pages – can be envisaged as diametrically opposed. The values of creativity, personal growth, subjective response, or radical social critique, in various combinations and with varying emphases, may be seen as antithetical to the grind of examinations and grading. And indeed it has become almost a commonplace that in the current English curriculum, the assessment tail wags the curriculum dog; that it matters little how creative or subversive English teachers are if in the end their subject is policed and assessed by reductive and mechanistic means. It seems to me there is much validity in this argument, and yet it need not be like that, and I have here chosen extracts which offer both critique and possibility: more humane modes of assessment sensitive at once to pupils, their teachers, the needs of the world beyond school, and – certainly not least – to the peculiarities of the subject English.

Sources

1.1 D'Arcy, P. (1995) *Two Contrasting Paradigms for the Teaching and Assessment of Writing*. Sheffield: NATE/NAAE.

1.2 Goodwyn, A. (1995) *English and Ability*. London: David Fulton.

1.3 Marshall, B. (2011) *Testing English: Formative and Summative Approaches to English Assessment*. London: Continuum.

1.4 Marshall, R. (2009) Epistemic Vagueness and English Assessment: Some Reflections, *English in Education* 43.1, 4–18.

1.5 Reed, M. (2004) Write or Wrong? A Sociocultural Approach to Schooled Writing, *English in Education* 38.1, 21–38.

1.6 Robinson, M. and Ellis, V. (2000) Writing in English and Responding to Writing, in J. Sefton-Green and R. Sinker (eds) *Evaluating Creativity: Making and Learning by Young People*. London: Routledge.

Introduction

Interestingly, the main emphasis in much of the commentary on assessment in English is on the assessment of *writing*, despite its status as just one of three attainment targets in the National Curriculum, and the huge emphasis in recent years on speaking and listening and on officially sponsored improvement of reading standards through the National Literacy Strategy and its descendants. Ultimately, most assessment of English expertise and attainment, through the formal examination system and otherwise, focuses on writing – perhaps, indeed, precisely because it is (or seems) the easiest mode to assess. The writers represented here look particularly at pupils' writing and its assessment, but not in isolation from other aspects of language use. Pat D'Arcy's short, but impressively clear-sighted, book argues for the linguistic, formal characteristics of writing assessment to be complemented by the process paradigm accentuating meaning and engagement. Published in 1995, in response to early manifestations of the National Curriculum, her arguments are, if anything, even more relevant today. Andrew Goodwyn builds on such perceptions, making the case for positive recognition of contextual features of writing in its assessment, especially in terms of coursework as opposed to final examination methods. Muriel Robinson and Viv Ellis look at assessment of writing in the context of educational creativity, again implicitly building on D'Arcy's work on the process-based paradigm. Further critiques are mounted by Richard Marshall and Malcolm Reed, while simultaneously offering positive alternatives to the officially sanctioned systems of assessment. Finally, in an important recent book focusing entirely on assessment in English with both critical rigour and realistically guarded optimism, Bethan Marshall presents a workable synthesis of approaches.

Extract 1.1

For the past decade, effectively since the advent of the National Curriculum, the way that teachers have been required to approach the teaching and the assessment of writing has become increasingly circumscribed within a narrowly mechanistic framework. It is bound by a paradigm which focuses on writing largely as a matter of construction and correctness – at word level, sentence level and text level. This kind of linguistic analysis is mechanistic because it pays little or no attention to the meaning of any specific piece of writing. Instead it restricts itself to generalisations about aspects of composition such as structure, organisation, spelling and punctuation.

My second paradigm is one that commanded considerable support in the teaching profession and generated much research throughout the 1980s. It focuses on writing as a mental activity. It is a process-based paradigm centred on a meaning-related approach both to how a text is constructed through the thoughts and feelings of the writer and also how a text is interpreted through the thoughts and feelings it evokes in the mind of a reader.

However, as teachers have prepared schemes of work for writing based on the statutory requirements in the Orders for English, and as they have been presented with the criteria for assessing pupil writing set out in the KS2 and KS3 SATs, I have heard no voices raised or seen nothing in print to ask what has happened to this perception of writing as a creative process of the mind, intent on making meaning. It is as though this second paradigm for writing has vanished without trace beneath the weight of a steady and relentless spate of official publications.

Of course, these paradigms are not mutually exclusive. The medium in which thoughts and feelings emerge from the mind of the writer is that of language, words arranged in a variety of patterns which take shape in a variety of forms both literary and non-literary. Nevertheless, those words could not arrive on page or screen unless they had been generated in the first place by the thoughts and feelings, the values and concerns, the knowledge and the understanding of the writer. Thinking activates language and written language renders thinking visible.

The difference between the two paradigms is crucially a matter of focus. An approach based on the first paradigm looks at the words on the page and at the patterns they make as words chain into phrases, clauses, sentences and paragraphs. An approach based on the second paradigm looks **through** the words on the page in order to construct the meanings which between them the words evoke.

[. . .]

Complex thinking and powerful feelings generate complex and powerful forms of language. At present I believe that we are in danger of approaching the bond between semantics and linguistics from the wrong direction – assuming that if we teach children grammatical patterns at word, sentence and text levels, they will learn to think more extensively. I suggest that we urgently need to rediscover and to have acknowledged in future official publications, a concept of writing as a process grounded in the search for meaning. A mechanistic paradigm which focuses primarily on construction and correctness, lacks those seeds of growth which this second paradigm would supply.

[. . .]

The problem is that there is this great black hole, more by omission than commission, where aspects of writing which relate to my second paradigm, are either ignored, or only receive lip-service bereft of back-up. There is no recognition that writing is a mental activity before it emerges as text, or that pupils possess the capacity to generate language and shape it at the point of utterance. The constant references to aspects of construction focus attention solely on a pupil's writing as an object for linguistic analysis at the expense of considering the meaning that every text produced by an individual writer seeks to convey.

There is no reference in any of these publications to writing 'from the inside', from that reservoir of recollections and speculations which are already a part of children's lives, related to their cultural experiences and to the values they hold. A recognition that writing can be an opportunity for personal creativity and reflection is submerged, as the attention of both teachers and pupils is constantly directed *outwards* to the genre forms that the texts of other writers demonstrate. Unfortunately, there is nothing in these final polished texts to indicate the meaning-related processes of writing which their authors experienced, before they were satisfied with what they had written. Instead, there is the assumption that if pupils analyse these constructs, they will learn how to produce excellent writing for themselves.

Extract 1.2

Ability in English is about the development of the individual in a social and cultural context and cannot be reduced to less than this complex interaction. The subject of English is concerned with human beings' collective and individual use of language, something that is constantly changing and developing. It is inevitably, and properly, much easier to understand how well a child is developing as a language user through monitoring that development over time but without impeding it by being over concerned with products. Someone who has ability in English has the capacity to receive and produce language with an increasing awareness of that language and of his or her individual relationship to it.

Similarly, assessment in English is by subjective individuals who draw on personal and collective expertise to reach agreements about the progress individuals have made and maintained and usually demonstrated through reading, writing, speaking and listening. Most public examining in English up until the advent first of CSE and then GCSE had depended on the simplistic notion that if you send a pupil's examination answers to an English teacher who does not know the pupil, then that assessor's judgement will be highly objective. All it is is anonymous! That judgement is then cross-checked by another judgement and then either confirmed or altered. A social factor in all this is that examiners undertake their task for piece-work payments, usually at the exhausted end of the academic year and to meet incredibly tight deadlines.

The original GCSE system, using 100% coursework, had modified this system so the initial teacher's original judgements were then moderated within the institution by another colleague who knew the context, i.e. who had valuable local knowledge to employ in making judgements. These two judgements were then moderated by another teacher external to the school as a part of a sample of schools, that moderator having the power to insist on changes to all grades from the school. In other words if the school was too soft or too hard, or simply inconsistent, they might affect the results of all their pupils. This was real collective responsibility.

This was not a perfect system because there cannot be one but it did combine the element of objectification with the powerful addition of contextual knowledge. It also achieved two remarkable and positive changes. First, it demystified examining to teachers and pupils; it was an open and understood process. Second, it created a wealth of assessment expertise in every school. As all teachers could be involved, so they were becoming increasingly clear about what they valued in a pupil's progress and this could connect to their teaching. This practise in refining subjective judgement was having a beneficial effect on good practice in the classroom. The steady rise in GCSE results in English and in pupils staying on to study the subject, suggests that standards were genuinely rising during the period of greatest teacher involvement in the assessment of English.

It becomes increasingly clear then that ability in English is not so much a problematic concept as a valuably complicated concept. English teachers themselves are quite happy with a holistic and broad approach to assessment which they see as vital if it is to be possible to assess pupils' ability in English and to reward their individual achievements. Examinations and tests are very limited and limiting and do not provide a broad, holistic framework for assessment.

Extract 1.3

So what then do we have? We have a subject which is all about judgement and choice. And this, in turn, means that it is about assessment. People who are good at English judge or assess almost everything. They assess whether the book they are reading is any good or whether the film they have just seen gripped them. They consider the style and form of what they have read and think about the visual grammar of a television programme. They may discuss a particular character or debate the central theme of a novel, but in doing so they are judging whether or not the writer had captured what it was they were trying to say. They examine adverts, even the back of cereal packets and what is more they assess what they themselves have written. Did they use the right word; was their expression cumbersome or that paragraph too long? All this they ask but they never stop assessing the quality of the text. People who are good at English assess.

Yet when asked to assess formally, English teachers baulk. For one thing they differ in their judgements. I may think that the novels of Jane Austen are divine, someone else may feel that they are the voice of a nineteenth-century woman talking of little else but local gossip. Then there is the problem that English, if it is to be considered an art, is not rule-bound and English teachers have a tendency to want to consider the whole of a piece rather than look at its constituent parts. This lands them in difficulties with most exam syllabuses. There is the problem, too, that most summative assessment does not capture all that a pupil does. They only select a small portion of what they can do And finally there is the problem that pupils are people who develop eccentrically. For many it is difficult constantly to assess a person's performance, always to think that there is something else they could do.

The question above all is how we put these two things together reliably? How do we get people, who assess everything they see to make judgements about pupils' work both formatively and summatively? Over the course of this book we hope to find out how some teachers have addressed this problem. For it should be remembered that understanding English as a language art enhances our standing within arts education in general. As Eisner wrote,

Work in the arts is not only a way of creating performances and products; it is a way of creating our lives by expanding our consciousness, shaping our dispositions, satisfying our quest for meaning, establishing contact with others and sharing a culture. (Eisner, 2002, p. 3)

[. . .]

What then do we learn from the turbulence that marks out English and assessment. The main thing is hope. Despite over a 150 years of battle English teachers are still trying to assess English in a way that makes sense to them. Confronted with 'A [department] of facts and calculations . . . With a rule and a pair of scales, and the multiplication table always in [their] pocket, sir, ready to weigh and measure any parcel of human nature' (Dickens, 1854, 1980, p. 10) they will always seek to develop the world of creativity and imagination.

From the battles with the London Board through the confrontation with the government over Sats English to the trials with KOSAP or Durham, English teachers will ask whether or not the government, of whatever hue, or the exam boards, or the QCDA have got it right. What keeps them going is the hope that one day someone will listen and say 'You may have got a point'.

Briefly, in the great scheme of things, on occasion they have. The trials that were started by the JMB in the 60s, which lasted for about 25 years, and ended with a 16+ exam, which assessed everybody, went someway to producing a holistic assessment in English for all. Continual complaints about the basics, the internet and cheating have got in the way. Now teachers have to grapple with controlled conditions exams and APP in a way that makes it hard to remember why they taught English in the first place.

Like so many of the teachers in this book my first real love is language – its rhythms and cadence, its capacity to create meaning for the author and audience alike. It is about English as an art. No matter how the functional is taught, or the basics covered the wonders of English cannot be fitted in to a tick box on correctness. But how such a love is to be taught is quite another matter – it requires rigour and thought. It needs Dewey's 'high organisation based upon ideas' (Dewey, 1966, pp. 28–9). But, 'To be truly artistic, a work must be aesthetic – that is framed for enjoyed receptive perception' (Dewey, 2005, p. 49).

Dewey, J. (1938; 1966) *Experience and Education*. London: Collier.

Dewey, J. (1934; 2005) *Art as Experience*. New York: Perigree.

Dickens, C. (1854; 1980) *Hard Times*. Harmondsworth: Penguin.

Eisner, E. (2002) *The Arts and the Creation of Mind*. New Haven, CT: Yale University Press.

Extract 1.4

Most things we want to assess in an English exam will mean teachers are confronted with ineradicable vagueness. This means that there have to be arbitrary decisions made with borderline cases. Instead of trying to simplify away vagueness by making exam criteria spuriously precise by treating vague terms as if they were precise (as if, for example, we were to stipulate that 'tall' means 'precisely six feet and over') exam systems should acknowledge the existence of vagueness and ensure that there is neither too much nor too little of.

There has to be arbitrariness in decisions being made, based on ignorance of what the evidence actually proves. But that shouldn't prevent teachers from being confident that in most of the cases they assess they can and do make the correct decision. The fact that there are some C grades a teacher can't know, doesn't mean that all the other cases s/he does know are for that reason suspect. Taught English is an incredibly complex and sophisticated subject. Evidence for success is often complex and difficult, not at all like assessing the sprint. But this isn't a problem. A competent teacher of English knows what a good essay on Macbeth is when s/he sees one, even though assessing the essay requires judging a huge variety of incommensurates, ambiguities, immensurates and other sources of complication. Sometimes there are essays that s/he doesn't know whether it's good or not, because they are borderline cases of good/not good essays. Vagueness captures this deep problem, but does so in a way that rejects total skepticism. We know the meaning of what we are saying and judging, it's just that there are some cases where our knowledge is too inexact to discriminate between correct and incorrect application. It's the human condition and assessment systems that should try and live with it, rather than pretend that we can engineer perfect knowledge of a candidate's performance, an attitude that stems from perhaps an overly deferential view of a scientific paradigm.

We shouldn't wallow in vagueness, however. Assessment systems need to minimise vagueness because they should minimise arbitrariness. But they should approach this in ways that don't distort what is being assessed by stipulating vagueness away. One way of doing this would be to just reduce the number of times vagueness is going to be confronted for high stakes. The fewer times there are high stakes assessments, the fewer times there are going to be arbitrary decisions with high stakes attached. Similarly, the fewer grade boundaries there are then the fewer arbitrary decisions are required. Complimenting this, the competency of assessors should be maximised by requiring that experts test out their powers of discrimination in *difficult* cases. (For example, look at the *platypus* (an animal with fur and a beak) to hone the discriminations surrounding 'mammal/bird' rather than a *hound*.) Such testing, through familiar mechanisms such as moderation meetings, should become essential to the profession. Subject knowledge too should be at a premium, in order that as broad a construct of the subject as is possible be available to such communities.

This will mean that complicated evidence can be presented and the knowledge of the assessors will be good enough most of the time for the evidence to be used to draw safe inferences. However, there should be the recognition that there will be cases where competent assessors don't know what inference they should draw from evidence presented, because these are borderline cases. But it's better that some cases be resolved arbitrarily, if the price of not doing so is to engineer systems that both diminish the role of competent practitioners from wrestling with the deep issue of their own subject matter, and which are equally arbitrary and which lead to inauthentic assessments. Such a system is what Royce Sadler's work on 'guild knowledge' seems to enjoin (Sadler, 1989), and which the NEAB 100% coursework model for English and English Literature GCSE back in the 1980s instantiated (QCA, 2004).

QCA (2004) *GCSE English Literature Review of Standards 1980–2000*. London: QCA.
Sadler, D. (1989) *Formative Assessment and the Design of Instructional Systems*. London: ASE.

Extract 1.5

> *And my lament/Is cries countless, cries like dead letters sent*
> (Hopkins, 1918, poem 45)

Sociocultural discussion of assessment promotes 'the Vygotskian position that education should lead development rather than follow it' (Kozulin, 1998, 53). Activities 'are aimed at developing a *dynamic position* [original emphasis] in the child, that is, the ability to approach objects and processes from different positions' (p.47). In the classic Vygotskian insistence that development should run ahead of the learner and be appropriated through symbolic interaction with a constructive peer or assessor and assessee, it is the material script that serves as text in this relationship. The script is neither the beginning nor the end of the activity system but a site with a potential for reciprocal action. The script is a complex (or node) of utterance in which, and through which, a writer's individual and cultural intentions and actions are formed and remembered, encountered and re-encountered, as the writer draws on both macro and micro-cultural and historical experiences in a specific learning context and through specified activity. To put it bluntly, one can conceive of few more complex interstices of 'culture in the middle' (Cole, 1985, 1996), or of 'genre as a cultural artefact' (Miller, 1994).

Cole, M. (1985) 'The Zone of proximinal development' in Wertsch, J (ed) *Culture, Communication and Cognition: Vygotskian Perspectives*. Cambridge: Cambridge University Press.

Cole, M. (1996) *Cultural Psychology*. Cambridge, MA: Harvard University Press.

Kozulin, A. (1998) *Psychological Tools*. London: Harvard University Press.

Miller, C. (1994) Genre and social action, in Freedman, A. and Medway, P. (eds) *Genre and the New Rhetoric*. London: Taylor & Francis.

Extract 1.6

What we have argued in this chapter is that there has been a tradition (which continues) of emphasis in school approaches to writing on form and structure rather than message and meaning. As a result, teachers have a traditional set of protocols and the accompanying metalanguage to enable them to give children explicit and detailed feedback on these aspects of their writing. Recent developments in our understanding of the nature of the writing process have led to a greater awareness of what these protocols need to be, and they have been refined and developed as a result of the work of whole language research, including the National Writing Project, and of the work of the genre theorists, in particular through the EXEL project in this country. The development of the National Curriculum and, more recently, of the National Literacy Strategy, has supported these protocols and placed great public value on form and structure in children's writing.

We have also shown how teachers have for many years also been aware of the need to give children space to write about what matters to them and have been excited by the times when children have produced writing which has a real sense of authorial voice and a powerful set of meanings, but that there has been no explicit metalanguage available to most teachers to give children explicit feedback on their work to help them develop this sense of voice and ability to convey their personal meanings more powerfully. In part, this comes from the traditional privileging of reading (reception) over writing (transmission) within English which has made most teachers more confident readers than writers and which has rarely created opportunities for the exploration of a reading-writing continuum. Since most teachers have not been and are not writers they have little personal experience to draw on and this exacerbates the lack of explicit protocols.

We have argued that the process-writing paradigm, which offers the potential for the development of more explicit protocols, has itself had to compete with other paradigms which are more in line with the establishment emphasis on form and structure, and so has largely failed to realise its potential, particularly in England. Paradoxically, its fascination with the developmental nature of spelling and structure has led to this paradigm too helping to develop and extend response protocols which focus extensively on structure.

However, we have also argued that there are ways forward which are already in evidence and which are compatible with current national policy and strategy. We have shown how reading workshops and literature circles have the potential to help children and teachers develop response protocols and mutually supportive strategies which can be translated into the writing situation. We have shown how publishing children's own work has an influence in bridging the reading–writing divide and allowing links to be made between response to commercially-published and classroom-produced texts. We have argued that the new electronic forms of publishing, including news-groups, have a particular potential to shift the power relationships between teacher and student. Where such developments are included in the initial teacher training experience, they have a particular role in helping future generations of teachers to have a more appropriate metalanguage and an explicit set of protocols for responding to all aspects of their pupils' writing. The responsibility then rests to a large extent to those of us involved in initial and continuing professional development for teachers to continue to re-assess our own practice so that more appropriate ways of facilitating and responding to the production element of English will become regular practice.

Exploratory questions

■ Consider the extracts above in the light of your own personal (as assessed) and professional (as teacher/assessor) experiences and observations: how do the views expressed accord with your recollections?

■ Pat D'Arcy especially is concerned here about the nature of writing and its assessment; try reflecting on your experience as a *writer*, exploring whether her perceptions strike a chord.

- What modes of assessment strike you as being particularly appropriate to the subject English, across the attainment targets (speaking and listening, reading and writing)? Is it helpful that the three areas be separated at all?
- Formative and summative modes of assessment are often seen as opposed to each other; need they be? As implied by some of the writers included here, especially Bethan Marshall, could they not rather be seen as complementary?
- Notions of formative assessment in English (and throughout the curriculum) have been accepted widely, and implemented through schemes of work and modes of practice; inevitably, however, the question is raised about profundity – is such assessment actually probing the depth of learning, as intended, or does it tend to remain superficial in practice?
- In various ways, all the extracts included here are critical of the current (and recent historical) situation regarding assessment in English, yet as teachers we have to work within the system: are there ways of managing any apparent contradictions here? Are there, indeed, things to be said for the current (arguably) assessment-heavy curriculum?

Further reading

As may be seen at a glance, the work of Paul Black and Dylan Wiliam has been greatly influential in guiding those concerned with education towards an appreciation of the complexities of assessment in theory and practice, and the possibilities of developing formative assessment practices in particular. Indeed, many of the writers represented in the extracts above, such as Bethan Marshall (also represented in a succinct NATE booklet in the list below), have been much influenced by Black and Wiliam's work and have sought to apply it specifically to English. Their 1998 and 1999 pamphlets (*Inside the Black Box* and *Beyond the Black Box*) effectively set the ball rolling, and are both succinct and eminently readable; their work with colleagues (especially the 2003 book *Assessment for Learning: Putting it into Practice*) interestingly developed the central arguments in a practical context of schooling, while Dylan Wiliam's collaboration with Bethan Marshall (*English inside the Black Box*, 2006) refers the issues directly to English. Other key commentators represented here include Colin Harrison, who was instrumental as both instigator and critic of the National Strategy (especially critical of its assessment dimension), and Mike Fleming, who illustrates here both a practical classroom-based exploration (2011) and a European dimension (2007). I have also included in this list a helpful survey of education issues, including the nature of assessment (Ian Davies and colleagues), and Sefton-Green and Sinker's exploration of assessment in the context of creativity in education – much of which pertains to English. Keogh et al. focus on English in their book, directly relevant to the needs of the classroom practitioner, while Debra Myhill and Philip Pullman, in strikingly contrasting ways, defend what they see as good practice in English pedagogy in the light of what could be construed as an assessment-driven curriculum.

Black, P. (1998) *Testing: Friend or Foe? Theory and Practice of Assessment and Testing.* London: Falmer Press.

Black, P. and Wiliam, D. (1998) *Inside the Black Box* (occasional paper). London: King's College.

Black, P. and Wiliam, D. (1999) *Assessment for Learning: Beyond the Black Box.* Cambridge: University of Cambridge School of Education.

Black, P., Harrison, C., Lee, C., Marshall, B. and Wiliam, D. (2003) *Assessment for Learning: Putting it into Practice.* Maidenhead: Open University Press.

Davies, I., Gregory, I. and McGuinn, N. (2002) *Key Debates in Education.* London: Continuum.

Fleming, M. (2007) *The Challenges of Assessment within Language(s) of Education.* Council of Europe (Strasbourg) conference paper: www.coe.int/lang (accessed 15 February 2011).

Fleming, M. (2011) Assessment, in M. Fleming and D. Stevens (eds) *English Teaching in the Secondary School.* London: Routledge.

Harrison, C. (1995) The Assessment of Response to Reading: Developing a Post-Modern Perspective, in A. Goodwyn (ed.) *English and Ability.* London: David Fulton.

Harrison, C. (2002) *The National Strategy for English at Key Stage 3: Roots and Research.* London: DFES.

Keogh, B., Dabell, J. and Naylor, S. (2008) *Active Assessment in English.* London: Routledge.

Marshall, B. (2004) *English Assessed.* Sheffield: NATE.

Marshall, B. and Wiliam, D. (2006) *English inside the Black Box: Assessment for Learning in the English Classroom.* London: NFER Nelson.

Myhill, D. (1999) Writing Matters: Linguistic Characteristics of Writing in GCSE English Examinations, *English in Education* 33.3, 70–81.

Pullman, P. (2002) *Perverse, All Monstrous, All Prodigious Things.* Sheffield: NATE.

Sefton-Green, J. and Sinker, R. (eds) (2000) *Evaluating Creativity.* London: Routledge.

7 Linguistic and cultural contexts

The essence of language study is, predictably enough, language itself – but this is where the controversy starts. Previous chapters have already served to illustrate this point from a range of perspectives, and in Chapter 7 we look with sharper focus at some views of language in education. The dynamic relationship between such differing (but also in many instances complementary) standpoints should emerge clearly, as should an enhanced appreciation of the practical teaching and learning possibilities of the English classroom.

Part 1: The workings of language

Sources

1.1 Allen, D. (1987) *English, Whose English?* Sheffield: NAAE.
1.2 Mittins, B. (1988) *English: Not the Naming of Parts.* Sheffield: NATE.
1.3 Myhill, D. (2011) Living Language, Live Debates: Grammar and Standard English, in J. Davison, C. Daly and J. Moss (eds) *Debates in English Teaching.* London: Routledge.
1.4 Perera, K. (1987) *Understanding Language.* Sheffield: NAAE.

Introduction

At a time of huge and long-reaching changes in the English curriculum and the practices of its teaching – the mid- to late-1980s – commentators such as David Allen, Bill Mittins and Katharine Perera went to some lengths in their appeal for sanity in curricular and pedagogical approaches to native language teaching. Today's English curriculum bears the scars, some more healed than others, from this embattled time – which is why I have included the extracts here. In the face of conservative appeals for legislation to force the 'education establishment' to teach traditional values, including a narrow and exclusive vision of grammar and Standard English (the subjects English and history were, arguably, the most contentious and controversial in this context), linguists and teachers called for rather different approaches. Bill Mittins, for instance, entitled his influential booklet, excerpted from here, *Not the Naming of Parts*, in opposition to the purely analytical teaching of language, separated from its contexts of actual use. He argued instead for a genuinely creative synthesis of approaches, dispelling widely held myths concerning the nature of language while so doing. Similar critiques may be found in the work of David Allen and Katharine Perera, celebrating language diversity and its inherently fascinating qualities. More recently, Debra Myhill reminds us powerfully that the debates are still very much 'live'; indeed their relevance to current English classrooms is today even more urgent than it was two decades ago.

Extract 1.1

Language is the creation and communication of meaning. Through language we remember the past, experience the present, and predict and plan the future. We experience the lives of others through language and give them accounts of our own. Through literature we extend these encounters so that we learn, and convey to others, lives, events and feelings beyond the limits of our daily world. Our own use of language is the nearest representation of ourselves that we commonly have. By their reaction to our words, others can hurt or heal us, foster or diminish us.

Language gives us the ability to acquire knowledge, solve problems and give meaning to our existence. It forms an essential part of the process by which societies are formed and perpetuated. Individuals learn meanings from social situations in which they take part. Ultimately they pass on these meanings to others. A large part of our lives in society is therefore spent in making, communicating or receiving meanings. Where this exchange of messages is lively and vital it is inevitable that both meanings and language change a little. This is a healthy sign of vigorous and enabling language and of a society which is self-aware and questioning.

The capacity of language for social cohesion can also, unfortunately, be used to manipulate, dominate and oppress. No language exists which is culture- and value-free, precisely because it always derives from the interchange of meanings in a particular culture. Language comes to us always coloured by the thoughts and feelings of previous users. Using language effectively means choosing carefully between examples and uses so that what is communicated is as far as possible what is intended. Good language users must know their audiences almost as well as they know themselves.

No distinction can be made between how children and adults learn language. Both learn through use in social situations, even though those situations may sometimes be represented by an audience distanced by print. Both also use language in order to learn, to record and classify information, identify and solve problems and explore and transform feelings. Neither the learning of language nor learning through language can be taught outside the context. However, children will increasingly be able to realise their own capacity in language where teachers can provide enabling experiences and sensitive intervention based on an understanding of what language is and how it works.

The main job of the teacher responsible for the growth and development of pupils' language is to enable the child to speak, listen, read and write effectively. To do this successfully, teachers need to organise the learning in ways which follow on logically and consistently from the successful language learning which children have already accomplished in the context of their own homes and communities: learning to speak their parents' language, whether that be English or any other first language. This means that school learning must retain the essential features of this learning, which are:

1. A very high expectation of success for the learner.
2. An "apprenticeship" approach to acquiring written and oral language, in which the adult represents the "success" the child seeks and yet offers endless help.
3. Maximum encouragement and support while errors are mastered.
4. Motivation for the learner to make sense of and acquire control over language and the power which it can have.
5. A constant respect for the child's language.

The teacher is also a learner, though more experienced, and the learner will benefit from occasions when she/he is given the opportunity to be the expert.

113

Thus the learner needs

> expectation of success,
>
> the confidence to take risks and make mistakes,
>
> a willingness to share and to engage,
>
> the confidence to ask for help,
>
> an acceptance of the need to readjust,

and the teacher needs

> respect for and interest in the learner's language culture, thought and intentions,
>
> the ability to recognise growth points, strengths and potential,
>
> the appreciation that mistakes are necessary to learning,
>
> the confidence to maintain breadth, richness and variety, and to match these to the learner's interests and direction (ie to stimulate and challenge), a sensitive awareness of when to intervene and when to leave alone.

What should children know about language?

Is it **knowledge** about language that our children need? Isn't it rather **understanding** of language and **control** over language, both of which will include the systematic acquisition of terms – but this should be subservient to experience and use of language. Experience precedes precept and analysis should follow competence. A lot of effort is wasted if the conceptual framework and terminology are introduced too early; if it is used to criticise a child's own expression it will be positively harmful. A vast amount of the knowledge we have about language is not made explicit either to ourselves or to others. Much of it should and will remain inexplicit; there seems to be some that can usefully be brought out in such a way as to add to the interest in language and even to the control of one's own language. Much of the knowledge included under the head of "traditional grammar" has a double disadvantage – it does not help **understanding** and it has no impact on **control**. What does seem to help control is a systematic exploration of language in situ, an examination through close attention to how language matches (or doesn't) its situation. This often draws attention to language elements larger than the sentence, which traditionally has been the focus of explicit attention – for example, language in group discussion, language in persuasion, language of those in authority.

Extract 1.2

The relationship between thought and language has been described as 'the deepest problem of the philosophic mind'. The old question (attributed variously to a schoolboy, a little girl, W. H. Auden, and doubtless others) of "How do I know what I mean until I hear what I say?" uses simpler words to express the same dilemma. It baffles most thinkers, from children to philosophers, but apparently not the Queen's English Society. . . . Their petition to Kenneth Baker is introduced with a single sentence:

> Sir: To encourage the clear and accurate expression of meaning, we urge you to introduce the compulsory study of formal grammar, including parsing and sentence analysis, into the school curriculum and the syllabus for the General Certificate of Secondary Education in English Language.

Presumably 'formal grammar' is the grammar of forms and corresponds to what is commonly called 'traditional grammar' or 'trad gram'. This kind of grammar was routinely taught—especially in grammar schools—by teachers of English until the middle of the twentieth century. Since then, doubts about its academic respectability, its adequacy and its teachableness in schools—accompanied by a strong reaction in favour of *using* the language instead of *studying* it—have discredited trad gram. The well-known logical fallacy of 'post hoc ergo propter hoc' is demonstrated in the odd statistical fact that the salaries of clergymen in Cumberland used to correlate closely with the price of Canadian wheat. But the similar illogicality which assumes that the concomitant variation of (a) decline in the teaching of grammar and (b) an alleged deterioration in the quality of language-use has not prevented many people from taking it for granted that (a) has caused the effect of (b). The petition launched by the Q.E. Society embodies this 'crooked thinking' and, sadly, has already (late 1987) enlisted the signatures of well-known personalities and will surely recruit many more names.

The issue presented in such deceptively simple terms reduces an enormously complex thing (language) to a polarized binary choice between two positions. What the Bullock Report's title called 'a language for life' cannot reasonably be treated in this way. A much bigger stage needs to be set. The actors on that stage include teachers, students, language theorists and researchers spread over centuries both BC (not just 'before Chomsky') and after. Their expertise overlaps with psychology, sociology, communication theory, linguistics, and much else.

Many thinkers have explored the opposition between the indeterminacy and consequent instability of language and the human preference for stability. The fuzziness and the constantly changing character of word-meanings conflict with the illusion of a certainty that is assumed to be available. But absolute certainty, especially what Wittgenstein called 'subjective' certainty, justifying a feeling of certitude, is in fact unattainable. Young children need a feeling (even if only relative) because they need a measure of security. But, inevitably, as Julian Huxley puts it, 'We must learn to bear the burden of incertitude'. As teachers, we ought to accept Bertrand Russell's suggestion (slightly misquoted) that 'To teach how to live without certainty, and yet without being paralyzed by hesitation, is perhaps the chief goal of education in our day.'

The essential usefulness of language is that it enables us to break up the continuum of human experience. We segment experience by arresting its movement and allocating to it words and word-strings. Epigrammatically, and with reference to the teaching of reading, Frank Smith asserted neatly that 'All programs fractionate experience'. This process must to some extent falsify or misrepresent realities. The fact that language keeps moving and changing—sometimes its forms but more often its meanings—makes correspondence between words and thoughts less than perfectly precise. So be it.

Extract 1.3

[S]ome of the discourses in the grammar and language debate appear certainly irreconcilable: prescriptivist and descriptivist views of language are positioned as binary opposites, and linguists and politicians may never agree because their goals and purposes are different. But in practice, rather than being at opposite ends of a language spectrum, prescriptivist and descriptivist views of language are better thought of as a Venn diagram, with two overlapping circles. There are many instances where everyone, including linguists, would agree that there are rules governing the language, particularly in terms of word order and syntax. In many ways language *is* normative, otherwise we'd find it hard to understand each other. Equally, there are many aspects of language use in which a descriptive approach is more appropriate – the evolving patterns of texting and tweeting, for example. It is in the intersection of the two circles where the debate is contentious, where a prescriptivist will argue for a normative rule and a descriptivist will argue that language use is changing ('I was sitting/I was sat', for example).

Many English teachers and educationalists advocate a pluralist approach to teaching, one which values dialectal diversity but also acknowledges that giving learners access to Standard English may help them in gaining access to powerful discourses and powerful positions. It is important not to romanticise the emancipatory potential of teaching Standard English, just as it is equally important not to romanticise local dialects: speaking Standard English may be necessary in a global world but it is not sufficient to ensure access to power. That is a far more complex issue, influenced by many societal factors, of which dialect is only one. In the English classroom, this pluralist approach would involve comparing linguistic differences between regional and social dialects and examining social attitudes to them. It would embrace the richness of dialectal variations and the language potential this offers but also support students in code-switching to Standard English, where appropriate. The teaching of both Standard English and dialects would be embedded in critical analysis of language in use and explicit discussion of issues of language and power.

The role of grammar in the English curriculum is perhaps more ambivalent than Standard English. Linguists with a strong understanding of the English curriculum, such as Ronald Carter, have argued for the study of grammar as an end in itself, part of a broad and balanced language curriculum. Certainly, access to a metalanguage enables much more precise discussion and analysis of language; for example, analysing how talk varies in informal conversation between friends and in an interview situation or analysing how transitive and intransitive verbs differently position men and women in romantic novels. In such contexts, grammar is a tool in the English classroom for critical analysis of spoken and written text.

The more contentious issue is whether teaching grammar can support students in developing their own talk and writing. There is very little evidence that teaching grammar has a positive impact on writing development, though there is good evidence that linguistic analysis can provide valuable insights for teachers into developmental trajectories and patterns

(Perera 1984; Myhill 2008) which might inform teaching decisions. However, a study currently being undertaken at the University of Exeter is showing a significant positive impact (effect size 1.52) of contextualised grammar teaching on writing attainment. Unlike previous studies, this study adopted a meaning-centred approach to grammar and writing in which meaningful aspects of grammar where taught, relevant to the genre of writing under study. The focus in this study is not on addressing grammatical errors, but at opening up alternative grammatical possibilities for meaning-making and developing a repertoire based on choice and understanding.

No doubt the language debate will continue, but Crystal neatly summarises a resolution of the debate as one in which there is recognition that grammar, language and meaning are inextricably intertwined, and that understanding these inter-relationships is empowering:

> Grammar is the structural foundation of our ability to express ourselves. The more we are aware of how it works, the more we can monitor the meaning and effectiveness of the way we and others use language. It can help foster precision, detect ambiguity, and exploit the richness of expression available in English. And it can help everyone – not only teachers of English, but teachers of anything, for all teaching is ultimately a matter of getting to grips with meaning.
>
> (Crystal 2004: 24)

Crystal, D. (2004) 'A twenty-first century grammar bridge' in *Secondary English Magazine* June 2004.

Myhill, D. (2008) Towards a linguistic model of sentence development in writing, in *Language and Education* 22(5).

Perera, K. (1984) *Children's Writing and Reading.* Oxford: Blackwell.

Extract 1.4

I believe that one reason why reference to 'knowledge about language' provokes so much disagreement is that such knowledge can be of at least three different kinds, and it is not always clear which kind is being referred to.

First, there is the implicit knowledge that all native speakers have. This enables us to say that, 'Yesterday our team won the match' is a possible sentence, whereas★ 'Yesterday our team wins the match' is not; or that, 'She has bought a red car' is all right but ★'She has bought a car red' is not. The fact that we can confidently recognize the ungrammaticality of these sentences shows that we know which verb tense is appropriate with a given adverb, and what the order of adjectives and nouns should be. The important point, though, is that such knowledge does not depend on having the technical terminology for describing the language: speakers who reject ★'Yesterday our team wins the match' have an implicit knowledge of English verb tenses even if they cannot identify the verb in the sentence or say what tense it is. This example concerns the grammar of English but it would be equally possible to illustrate the point with reference to the vocabulary or sound system of the language. Secondly, there is explicit knowledge about the nature and functions of language: an understanding of how it is acquired, used and abused; of how and why it varies and changes; of how it can enchant or offend, manipulate or persuade or alienate. Thirdly, there is explicit knowledge of the structure of language – knowledge which includes the technical terminology necessary to describe the production and organization of speech sounds, the relationships of meaning between different words, and the grammatical structures of the language.

The three different kinds of knowledge about language are not rigidly separated from each other: our implicit knowledge of our mother tongue informs any study we make of it; an understanding of the way the language has changed over the centuries is bound to involve discussion of sounds, word meanings and grammatical structures; and so on. Nevertheless, lessons that are designed to develop an understanding of the nature and functions of language (sometimes referred to as 'language awareness' courses) will differ appreciably in their approach, methodology and terminology from lessons that aim to establish a systematic description of the phonology, semantics and grammar of English. For example, on the first type of course, secondary pupils could be led to an awareness that, while rhyme depends on a patterning of vowel sounds, alliteration arises from the repetition of consonant sounds. But it would only be on the second type of course that **definitions** of the terms 'vowel' and 'consonant' would be needed.

Another reason for some of the hostility from English teachers towards 'knowledge about language', I think, is that it is not always made clear that there is a difference between what teachers need to know about the language and what they need to teach. Therefore, the purpose of this paper is to try to outline what I believe all primary teachers and secondary English teachers need to know about language, and to suggest briefly what aspects of that knowledge might be of benefit to their pupils. I shall be concerned with an understanding of the nature and functions of language (the second of the three kinds of knowledge I identified earlier), but first I should like to digress to make a point about the academic study of language structure.

In *English from 5 to 16*, it is stated that, 'Learning *about* language is necessary as a means to increasing one's ability to use and respond to it; it is not an end in itself' (p. 14). This idea that teaching children about their own language is justified only if it leads to some kind of improvement in their linguistic behaviour is very wide-spread – and I find it rather odd. Language is an integral and fascinating part of our environment – every bit as important as the electric bell or fold mountains or the Spinning Jenny – and yet we require it to justify its place in the curriculum by demonstrating its practical usefulness. That seems, as Bloor (1979) has suggested, like telling biology teachers that they should not teach their pupils about the digestive system unless they can prove that doing so enables them to digest their food better.

When language study as an academic subject is well taught by knowledgeable teachers it can be very appealing to pupils; experience of the new Joint Matriculation Board 'A' level in English Language convinces me of that. One of the more surprising effects of this 'A' level course has been that it has given students a sense of pride in their own language. Apparently, many of them had felt that English was in some way inferior to French or German, believing that it lacked – in the words of one of them – 'verbs and grammar and that'. I understand that it has been a source of considerable satisfaction to discover that English does indeed have a grammar.

However, I do believe that the academic study of language, as an end in itself, requires (like any other academic subject) teachers who are specifically trained to teach it. I also think that it should be an optional subject, not an obligatory one, and that it is best suited to the upper years of the secondary school. So it is not that type of language study that I am focusing on in this paper; rather, it is the kind of language teaching that is part of the work of any primary teacher or secondary English teacher, as they strive to help their pupils increase their ability to use and respond to their mother tongue.

Exploratory questions

■ Over twenty years ago, the Kingman Committee set out to decide how much, and what kind of, grammatical/linguistic knowledge is needed to teach English as a native language; as texts throughout this compilation indicate, the debate continues – what is your view, based on professional experience?

- Assuming your response to the question posed above indicates that *some* such knowledge is necessary, how should this best be imparted to pupils? 'Not the naming of parts', says Bill Mittins, but what is the role, if any, of linguistic analysis?

- David Allen distinguishes between *knowledge* and *understanding* of language, favouring the latter; in a professional classroom-based context, is this a helpful distinction?

- Similarly, Katharine Perera carefully separates different aspects of knowledge about language, whilst acknowledging their ultimate unity; again, do you find such distinctions helpful in practice?

- Debra Myhill presents a possible synthesis of views on language teaching, here and elsewhere in her writing; does this reflect actual practice? Should it?

Further reading

Ronald Carter and David Crystal, eminent linguists both, continue to enjoy widespread and enthusiastic currency among the English teaching profession – and rightly so. Both are represented here by some of their insightful studies of language – not necessarily in distinctly educational settings, but certainly appropriate to the needs of the English classroom (and, ideally, the needs of the whole school). I have also included here three official reports: 'Bullock', presenting a framework for language across the curriculum; 'Kingman', as noted above seeking to explore what kind of knowledge about language is required for secondary schooling; and 'Cox', concerned to present the outline of the (then) relatively new National Curriculum for English. Each of these continues to be very influential. Stephen Pinker's book *The Language Instinct* gives English teachers a helpful theoretical context – to be approached critically, of course. I have also included works by Mittins, Ross and Cameron – all seeking to show how language affects the professional lives of teachers – English teachers especially – with different emphases. Finally, Teresa Grainger's edited *Reader* offers an impressive collection of papers and excerpts pertaining to language and literacy in international contexts.

Cameron, D. (2007) *The Teacher's Guide to Grammar.* Milton Keynes: Open University Press.

Carter, R. (1990) *Knowledge about Language and the Curriculum.* London: Hodder & Stoughton.

Carter, R. (1995) *Key Words in Language and Literacy.* London: Routledge.

Carter, R. and Nash, W. (1990) *Seeing through Language.* Oxford: Blackwell.

Crystal, D. (1987) *The Cambridge Encyclopedia of English*. Cambridge: Cambridge University Press.

Crystal, D. (1995) *The Cambridge Encyclopedia of the English Language*. Cambridge: Cambridge University Press.

Crystal, D. (2004) *Making Sense of Grammar*. London: Pearson Longman.

Crystal, D. (2004) *Rediscover Grammar*. London: Pearson Longman.

Dean, G. (2003) *Grammar for Improving Reading and Writing in the Secondary School*. London: Fulton.

DES (1975) *A Language for Life* (The Bullock Report). London: HMSO.

DES (1988) *Report of the Inquiry into the Teaching of English Language* (The Kingman Report). London: HMSO.

DES (1989) *English for Ages 5–16* (The Cox Report). London: HMSO.

Grainger, T. (ed.) (2004) *The RoutledgeFalmer Reader in Language and Literacy*. London: RoutledgeFalmer.

Mittins, W. (1990) *Language Awareness for Teachers*. Milton Keynes: Open University Press.

Pinker, S. (1994) *The Language Instinct: The New Science of Language and Mind*. London: Penguin.

Ross, A. and Hunt, P. (2006) *Language Knowledge for Secondary Teachers*. London: Fulton.

Part 2: Some cultural contexts of language in education

Sources

2.1 Sharwood-Smith, M. (2007) British Shibboleths, in E. Ronowicz and C. Yallop (eds) *English: One Language, Different Cultures*. London: Continuum.

2.2 Rosowsky, A. (2010) Writing It in English: Script Choices among Young Multilingual Muslims in the UK, *Journal of Multilingual and Multicultural Development*, 31.2,: 163–179.

2.3 Green, B. (1993) *The Insistence of the Letter: Literacy Studies and Curriculum Theorising*. London: Falmer Press.

2.4 Millard, E. (1997) *Differently Literate: Boys, Girls and the Schooling of Literacy*. London: Falmer Press.

Introduction

Clearly, language cannot exist in isolation from the contexts of its uses: the diversity of texts represented in this book, indeed, testifies to this truth. In Part 2 of Chapter 7, I include four writers who have commented on different aspects of language in context. Michael Sharwood-Smith looks at English in the UK from an international perspective, with particular emphasis on such thorny topics as Standard English and Received Pronunciation (RP). In a complex but ultimately revealing study, *The Insistence of the Letter*, Bill Green and contributors analyse the nature of language in the processes of education – clearly relevant to English teaching – from a radical Australian perspective. Andrey Rosowsky is concerned with language as practised by particular ethnic and religious groups within the UK, noting the developing relationship between such uses and mainstream English (as denoted, indeed, by such apparently straightforward terms as Standard English and RP). Elaine Millard, in her dynamically influential book *Differently Literate*, presents gender as a determining factor in the ways language is taught and learned in schools. All four writers represented here seek to demystify language in cultural contexts, whilst simultaneously espousing diversity.

Extract 2.1

In sum, as the British, and more specifically the English, look out from their particular part of a small island across to Australia and Canada and the USA and many other countries in between, they see 'their' language spoken far and wide in various forms and with various accents. These accents amuse and occasionally horrify them but nonetheless this variety of English has provided the British with the reassurance that it is not really necessary for them to learn a foreign language. More than that, the British can cling to the irrational but unsurprising notion that the 'true' form of English is the one spoken in the island where it originated.

The idea of a correct way of speaking English suggests that there is a single standard for all to follow. From afar, it might indeed seem that educated people in Britain all speak one kind of English. Watching British films might lead you to add a few non-standard options, perhaps Cockney, Liverpudlian, Scottish or Irish (depending on the films you watch). In reality, the majority of the inhabitants of the British Isles speak what might be called non-standard English. This is particularly true when it comes to accent. The standard British accent taught all over the world is RP (Received Pronunciation, see Chapter 2) but speakers of RP are a small minority in their own country. Nevertheless, RP is a widely understood accent, free of any regional association within England itself and spoken throughout the UK. It is the most exhaustively described accent in the English language and is still held up as the accent to aim at in many non-English-speaking countries. Within the UK, it is popularly associated with the royal family, the BBC and those who were educated at private schools.

The success of RP is that it is an accent that everyone understands – even though they might not speak it. When the BBC World Service first tried to make its English more representative of the country at large and introduced different accents into its news broadcasts, there was a chorus of complaints from listeners in other countries, and the BBC went back to RP.

If we take 'standard' to refer to grammar and vocabulary, and particularly to written English, not to pronunciation or accent, then the number of users of standard British English is quite large and may be said to include the majority of educated native speakers, whatever accent they happen to speak. As has been mentioned before, standard British English (but not including pronunciation) is really very close to educated English in North America and indeed to educated English around the world.

In spoken English, the various regions of the British Isles not only have local accents but also local vocabulary and idiom. It is therefore not surprising that people from, say, Fife in Scotland or Cardiff in south Wales or Cornwall in south-western England, may sound very different from each other. Not only foreigners but also people from other parts of Britain may have difficulty in understanding some local speech. The reality of Britain is far from the stereotype of a country bursting with RP speakers. And even RP speakers may betray regional traces. (See Chapter 2 for mention of Estuary English, a compromise between RP and local south-eastern accents.) Many people blend in to their accent enough of RP to sound educated and worthy of employment but not enough to be associated with the upper social class that RP traditionally represents.

Attitudes to accents change. The national accents – educated Welsh, Scots and Irish – have always been more socially acceptable in Britain, but since the 1960s the respectability of regional accents has grown considerably. As suggested above, many people even avoid a pure RP for fear of sounding snobbish or, if they are from outside England, 'too English'. Many non-native speakers of English are more conservative in this regard, and as learners are unlikely to be judged 'posh' for speaking RP. When actually visiting the UK, they still need to be prepared for constant exposure to accents that are not RP.

Immigration has made modern Britain a multilingual, multi-ethnic society, but it has always been so since English was first spoken there. Celtic languages, spoken in the British Isles before the arrival of the Germanic peoples who brought what was to become English, have continued to be spoken and survive in several areas. Welsh is enjoying a strong revival and there are even attempts being made to bring Cornish back to life. Moreover, Irish Gaelic (now known simply as Irish) is an official language of the Republic of Ireland. A small percentage of the population of Scotland speaks Scottish Gaelic (not to be confused with Scots, the Germanic language of the old Scottish court referred to earlier) and another closely related Gaelic language, Manx, is spoken on the Isle of Man. But English is of course the main language of the British Isles and is spoken as first language by the vast majority of the population.

Extract 2.2

This article seeks to describe and, to an extent, interpret a recently observed regular religioliteracy practice in which participants, mostly young, make recourse to roman script in their endeavours to record, memorise and share poetic verses and song lyrics composed in languages traditionally associated with non-roman scripts.

Specifically, there is resurgence in interest among young British Muslims in traditional poetry (*qasai'd, naat, ghazal*) and song (*nasheed*) composed principally in Urdu, Panjabi, Farsi, Bengali and Arabic. As the original scripts (Arabic, Perso-Arabic, Shahmukhi) for these texts are to a large extent unavailable to the young participants, when they wish to transcribe poems and songs, they employ the only script they know, the roman script. Certainly, many of them will have knowledge of the script, Arabic, used to decode the Qur'an but they will be predominantly passive users, reader/decoders rather than writers/transcribers. There is also some evidence in some UK mosque schools of teachers and resources employing roman script in the transliteration of the Classical Arabic alphabet and primers used to teach the decoding of the Qur'an. These two related sociolinguistic phenomena will be described in their local, situated (Barton, Hamilton, & Ivanic, 2000) contexts, but we will also seek to elucidate at all times those connections and influences, both linguistic and extra-linguistic – the political, the cultural, the historical, the economic, the pedagogical, the religious – that join these local events to more global and universal perspectives regarding scripts, their deployment and their associations with particular languages . . .

In the second incidence of script adoption, it is the need to write, or to transcribe, which is key. It is acknowledged in the literature that scripts can be 'powerful symbols of identity and cultural association' (Coulmas, 1989).

In the 'messy' multilingual and plurilingual and culturally dislocated contexts of Diasporas such considerations can appear a little way down the priority list. Harris (2006, p.6) refreshingly discusses multilingual practice in a London suburb as something 'everyday' and not something 'spectacular' or somehow salient. Language choices are often (usually?) made pragmatically drawing on individual and group linguistic resources to suit context rather than conscious and deliberate decisions reflecting ethnocultural allegiance. The example of script adoption cited here shares in this pragmaticism and this 'everyday-ness' as the young people involved draw upon the most useful and, crucially, uniquely available script, roman, to use for the transcription of their multilingual poetry and song.

This developing interest in and promotion of recitation, singing, collection and memorisation of religious poems which often trace their composition back hundreds of years, manifest themselves in the personal use of handwritten notebooks, transliterated publications, and in the resources of the internet. The latter, with its historical bias towards the English language, but even more so, towards roman script, is serving to reinforce and consolidate – and make familiar and normal – the use of roman script to transcribe Urdu, Panjabi and Arabic poetry and song.

These internet resources are very often plurilingual offering lyrics on songs and poetry originally composed in Arabic, Urdu, Farsi, Panjabi, Arabic and English, and, increasingly, in a combination of languages. The lyrics are transliterated exclusively in roman script. It would appear that, as yet, as far as these sites are concerned, there is no application of an agreed or conventional transliteration system (which does exist) with individual transliterators imposing their own interpretation of language and script based upon their own knowledge of the conventions of transcribing and spelling English. This is exacerbated when the transliterator is not, in fact, a 'transliterator' but a 'transcriber' and is transcribing from an oral knowledge of the song or poem directly into roman script. The scripts, then, represent a 'rough and ready' form of notation that contrasts with the more formal and often academic practice of accurate transliteration, which many young participants find over-complicated.

The idio-scripts (or more exactly – ideo-orthographies) thus created form part of this script community (Houston, 2008) that exists globally via the internet as well as locally. Idio-scripts are, of course, not unfamiliar to anyone with a passing acquaintance with SMS communications and are, one might safely predict, a vital part of electronic communications in the early part of the 21st century. Pétillon (2006) has drawn an interesting parallel between the latter development and the highly personal styles of medieval scribes suggesting that the idiosyncratic nature of texting or MSN communication makes for the development of 'idioscripts' and a return to the privatisation of writing and orthography.

There are two perspectives one can take when analysing this scriptal practice. A positive interpretation sees this as a 'bottom-up' authentic linguistic adaptation far removed from issues relating to national identity and political or cultural allegiance – more akin to the 'everyday' language practices described by Harris (Harris, 2006, p. 3) than to the 'spectacular' deliberateness of a socio-cultural choice. There are also potential positive spin-offs for mainstream educators in schools, particularly so with the use of roman script with younger children in the mosque school, as phoneme-grapheme correspondences based on the same script are consolidated and reinforced. It provides a way-in to heritage languages such as Panjabi and Urdu that sidestep difficulties with the script ('phrase book' Panjabi becomes a possibility). The use of roman script for Arabic, Urdu and Panjabi opens the door for more use of the English language and interaction with the majority culture and is a very visible example of cultural hybridity (Hutnyk, 2005).

A negative view of this literacy practice would be to interpret it as an aspect of language loss or shift, or more exactly, script loss or shift. Lack of acquisition of the scripts of heritage languages is not a 'neutral' or 'natural' linguistic phenomenon but a consequence of deliberate socio-economic and political decisions that are made in a context of power inequalities. The marginalised and economically deprived circumstances of the communities from which these young people come are determined by political and discursive decision-making, often tinged with racist and neo-colonial connotations. The lack of support for mother tongues other than English in UK society is well attested. This monolingual policy of British life and society influences all its principal institutions including schools.

Further research is needed to elucidate other examples of *scripta lingua francas* operating in a similar manner. The internet and its hitherto reliance on roman script, allied to the needs of Diaspora communites to maintain links both locally and globally, is a powerful influence on the 'naturalisation' of script adoption. Time will tell how permanent such usage is.

Barton, D., Hamilton, M. and Ivanic, R. (2000) *Situated Literacies: Reading and Writing in Context*. London: Routledge.

Coulmas, F. (1989) *The Writing Systems of the World*. Oxford: Blackwell.

Harris, C. (2006) *When is a First Language More Emotional?* London: Multilingual Matters.

Hutnyk, J. (2005) *Diaspora and Hybridity.* London: Sage.

Extract 2.3

One of the most important features of mass compulsory state-sponsored schooling has been the manner in which it has brought together what, in Foucault's terms, are disciplinary and pastoral forms of power. This has meant combining control and welfare concerns, on the one hand, and on the other, text-based forms of social management, on the level specifically of classrooms. It is something which has not been limited to the English subjects, either, although it might well be the case that pastoral power arrangements and technologies have been especially significant in the areas of literary education and English teaching. However, as Hamilton suggests in this volume, the textbook has long been a central organizing principle in general educational practice, and this is a matter which has become increasingly important over the course of the twentieth century, given the nexus between a multinational educational publishing industry and the professionalization of schooling (Apple, 1986; Luke, 1989). A related matter has been the general shift from 'speech' to 'writing' as the basis of formal education, which needs to be seen as crucial to the emergence and consolidation of modern schooling. This shift went together historically with a new valuation of silence in education and, increasingly, an official emphasis on reading and writing, rather than speaking and listening: 'reading and writing, rather than the more "natural" means of learning such as oral discussion and practical engagement, are the established modality of schooling' (Goodson and Medway, 1990: vii). Stressing the decline of interest in oral language, linked to the decline of traditional forms of education based on classical rhetoric, Christie (1990: 12) points to 'the related pedagogical requirement that children be educated in large numbers and disciplined to work in silence, a requirement which became commonplace in the nineteenth century, the period of mass education'. As she further writes, following Shirley Brice Heath: 'children were encouraged to talk less and less, while their progress was measured more and more through the written mode, a practice which survives today' (Christie, 1990: 15 . . .).

This 'silence' is certainly one aspect of the insistence of the letter in curriculum and schooling: that is, a programmatic emphasis on 'text' as the organizing and authorizing centre of one's attention and the source of one's educational identity, as it is and as it is becoming, and what it must eventually be — in short, an insistence *on* the letter. One way of grasping the significance of post-1960s efforts to restore the significance of speech in the practice of education, which Medway (1984) describes as analogous to the revolution associated with the translation of the Bible into the vernacular, was that it represented a major challenge to the normative ordering of modern schooling, emphasizing as this had long done the principles of hierarchy, linearity and what Hoskin (1979: 146) calls 'rational authority', together with the 'closed system' forms of thinking which Ong (1977) associates with the literacies and cultural technologies of writing and print. In a similar way, the shift from reading to writing, especially when associated with and linked to the new emphasis on speech, needs to be similarly reassessed, and viewed as constituting at least a *contradictory* politics.

Apple, M. (1986) *Teachers and Texts*. New York: Routledge and Kegan Paul.

Christie, F. (1990) *Literacy for a Changing World*. Hawthorn, Victoria: Australian Council for Educational Research.

Goodson, I. and Medway, P. (1990) *Bringing English to Order*. London: Falmer.

Hoskin, K. (1979) The examination, disciplinary power and rational schooling, in *History of Education* 8 (2).

Luke, A. (1989) 'Literacy as Curriculum' in *Language, Learning and Literacy* 1(2).

Medway, P. (1984) The Bible and the vernacular, in Britton, J. (ed.) *English Teaching: An International Exchange*. London; Heinemann.

Ong, W. (1977) *Interfaces of the World*. Ithaca NY: Cornell University Press.

Extract 2.4

There are two interconnecting frameworks within which to consider the ways in which teachers may work to change the literacy practices of their own classroom. The first of these is shaped by the current structure and classroom practices of the English or language curriculum. I shall suggest ways in which an over-emphasis on narrative, particularly fictional narrative, in the teaching of reading may be restructured to meet the developmental needs of both boys and girls. The second framework is the one constructed by the wider compass of the whole curriculum, which is taken to include an increasing range of educational practices attendant on the spread of the new technologies. The latter, I shall further suggest, make it imperative that schools re-examine current literacy practices in order to ensure greater access to a full range of experiences for all learners.

Redressing Imbalances

The first stage, then, is to consider how boys' and girls' reading interests may be more equally provided for within the current organization of their reading and writing time. Previous initiatives to redress gender imbalances in school subjects have been able to achieve significant changes in pupils' perceptions of themselves as competent learners. I am thinking in particular of the work of Walkerdine and Walden in the 1980s which drew teachers' attention to inequalities inscribed in the practice of mathematics teaching and encouraged the development of 'girl friendly' programmes of study (Walden and Walkerdine, 1985). Current evidence suggests that in most areas of the curriculum, up to the age of 16+, girls are well able to hold their own, if not surpass their male peers. Now the major cause for concern is schools' realization that boys are falling behind, particularly in the language curriculum. One possible reason for this, is that boys are not sufficiently engaged in the reading process, thereby missing out on an essential element of learning. My first suggestions, then, concern ways of adapting the current approach to reading in ways that are more 'boy friendly', without losing sight of practices that have enabled girls to succeed. Most of the following recommendations are aimed at promoting whole classes' range and motivation in reading, on the basis that boys will be prompted to take more interest in a topic that is given a high profile in the curriculum and where success is openly rewarded (West, 1986). There are some specific activities suggested, however, which draw on other kinds of reading identified by the research as of particular interest to large groups of boys. It will be up to the teacher to decide whether these are to be specifically targeted at boys in the class or shared with girls.

[. . .]

Schools need to recognize that a decline in sustained reading in leisure time is a feature of modern culture, equally applicable to the parents as to their adolescent children. This means that it cannot be assumed that pupils will encounter sufficient experience of continuous prose through reading at home. The Nottingham survey, and the work of Benton (1995), who concentrated his survey on the reading interests of 12–13-year-old pupils, corroborate my own findings, that the range of children's private reading has shrunk, with a concentration in the middle years on popular authors such as Roald Dahl or on series fiction, which make limited demands on understanding. If we continue to argue that stories carry within them the history of a particular culture and create a cross-hatching of cultural reference which depends on sustaining a reading of narrative, then we also need to acknowledge that most children need help in accessing more complex texts. Not only do children's individual preferences ignore large areas of reading, but the disparity between homes where book reading is encouraged and those where it rarely features increases pupils' inequality in access to a schooled literacy. Difference in exposure to reading increases with age, dropping off most heavily between the ages of 11–14. Junior schools, therefore, have a major role to play in ensuring that pupils have been introduced to a wide range of genres and formats as part of the experience of reading in school. Pupils' choice of reading at ages 8–11 requires the most careful monitoring so that secondary teachers are able to build on young readers' prior interests and enthusiasms.

Benton, M. (1995) *Studies in the Spectator Role.* London: RoutledgeFalmer.
Walden, R. and Walkerdine, V. (1985) *Girls and Mathematics.* London: Institute of Education.
West, A. (1986) The limits of discourse, in *English Magazine* (18).

Exploratory questions

- Linguistic and cultural diversity amongst pupils is sometimes presented in the media as a problem; need it be? Might it be, conversely, an opportunity for English teachers?
- How much regard for the international contexts of the English language should teachers of English as a native language have (in the various countries concerned)? How should this regard manifest itself in practice?
- Following Green, among many others, awareness of the crucial and critical role of language in education is growing; in what ways may this awareness influence English teaching specifically? Should English teachers necessarily take a lead in their schools in this respect?
- How important, in your own professional experience, is gender in the English teaching context? Should we be concerned to offer different approaches and texts to boys and girls? If so, are there dangers of playing to and thus reinforcing particular gender stereotypes?

Further reading

I have cast the net wide in selecting the following recommendations; not all of the works deal primarily with language, but they do all have important things to say about language, culture and education in various combinations and orders of priority. Some of the writers cited here have appeared elsewhere in the present book: Eagleton, Freire, Giroux, Lankshear and Rosen, for example, who here give radical commentaries on the nature of literacy and cultural change. Chomsky's work on the sociology of education, similarly radical, frequently touches on the centrality of language, as do the writings of the educational philosopher Ivor Goodson. I have included also pertinent books and papers by Glazier, concerned with justice and literacy education, Haslam et al., addressing English as an additional language in schools, Moore, considering specifically the teacher's role here, and Marsh and Millard, who explore literacy in terms of its relationship to popular culture.

Chomsky, N. (2003) *Chomsky on Democracy and Education*, ed. P. Otero. London: RoutledgeFalmer.

Eagleton, T. (2000) *The Idea of Culture*. Oxford: Blackwell.

Freire, P. and Macedo, D. (1987) *Literacy: Reading the Word and the World*. South Hadley, MA: Bergin & Garvey Publishers.

Giroux, H. (1997) *Pedagogy and the Politics of Hope: Theory, Culture and Schooling*. Boulder, CO: Westview Press.

Glazier, J. (2007) Tinkering towards Socially Just Teaching: Moving from Critical Theory to Practice, *Changing English* 14.3, 375–382.

Goodson, I. (2005) *Learning, Curriculum and Life Politics*. London: Routledge.

Goodson, I. and Medway, P. (1990) *Bringing English to Order*. London: Falmer Press.

Haslam, L., Wilkin, Y. and Kellet, E. (2006) *English as an Additional Language: Meeting the Challenge in the Classroom*. London: Fulton.

Lankshear, C. (1993) Curriculum as Literacy: Reading and Writing in 'New Times', in B. Green (ed.) *The Insistence of the Letter: Literacy Studies and Curriculum Theorising*. London: Falmer Press.

Lankshear, C. (ed.) (1997) *Changing Literacies*. Buckingham: Open University Press.

Marsh, J. and Millard, E. (2000) *Literacy and Popular Culture*. London: Paul Chapman.

Moore, A. (2000) *Teaching and Learning: Pedagogy, Curriculum and Culture*. London: RoutledgeFalmer.

Rosen, H. (1992) The Politics of Writing, in K. Kimberley, M. Meek and J. Miller (eds) *New Readings: Contributions to an Understanding of Literacy*. London: A & C Black.

8 Future possibilities and tensions concerning secondary English

In this book I have tried to represent a range of models of, approaches to and views on the subject English stretching back over the best part of a century. If one looks at the development historically, it is possible to interpret the subject as unfolding in a certain direction – although what precisely this direction is will inevitably depend on vantage point. Looking towards the future of the subject is even more problematic: do we take particular practices and trends currently discernible and extrapolate from them what the future may hold? If so, the pitfalls are many, not least in that these practices and trends are by no means universally discerned in the first place – this indeed is part of the message I am trying to convey in this book. And even if there is some shared understanding, it's not necessarily the case that the future will endorse what is currently thought or practised (a good example of this is the language across the curriculum model, which after Bullock was once widely thought to be the key to the future of English). It's also something of a truism, but perhaps containing a kernel of good sense, that there is a pendulum motion discernible in the development of educational practice and policy – but by the same token, it can be tricky to perceive exactly when the pendulum has swung to its fullest extent and what form its return over previous areas will take.

More importantly, I am also concerned about adopting an over-deterministic approach to future prospects: a sense that the future will happen come what may. Part of the purpose of this book, indeed, is to help equip beginning (and more experienced) English teachers with greater understanding of what has shaped our subject precisely so that we may knowledgeably play a part in how English unfolds. In the end, I hope we can agree with William

Blake, who wrote, 'Every honest man is a prophet; he utters his opinion both of private and public matters. Thus: if you go on so, the result is so. He never says, such a thing shall happen let you do what you will. A prophet is a seer, not an arbitrary dictator' (*Marginalia to Watson's Apology*). This formulation, as so often with Blake, gets to the heart of the matter: it is about empowerment, about what sort of life, or indeed what sort of English teaching, we want to see.

With this in mind, I have selected here five commentators who, it appears to me, do have important and challenging things to say about these future prospects. Richard Andrews here moves towards a conclusion to his exhaustive summary of research into English pedagogy, noting pertinent trends. Shirley Brice Heath writes in a similar vein, in her 'afterword' for an important (and previously encountered) book, broadening the social and political context in so doing. Gunther Kress and colleagues focus on the development of meaning-and-values as crucial to the future of the subject, echoed by Peter Medway in his lucid plea for endorsement of enlightenment principles, and indeed by Caroline Daly in her thoughtful assessment of what is important about new technologies as influences on English teaching and learning.

Sources

1.1 Andrews, R. (2001) *Teaching and Learning English: A Guide to Recent Research and Its Applications*. London: Continuum.

1.2 Brice Heath, S. (2007) 'Afterword', in V. Ellis, C. Fox and B. Street (eds) *Rethinking English in Schools: Towards a New and Constructive Stage*. London: Continuum.

1.3 Daly, C. (2011) The 'Real World' of Technologies: What Kinds of Professional Development Are Needed for English Teachers?, in J. Davison, C. Daly and J. Moss (eds) *Debates in English Teaching*. London: Routledge.

1.4 Kress, G. et al. (2005) *English in Urban Classrooms*. London: RoutledgeFalmer.

1.5 Medway, P. (2010) English and Enlightenment, *Changing English* 17.1, 3–12.

Extract 1.1

In the first chapter, the nature of English was considered. What emerged in the late 1980s and in the 1990s was that the subject English, in schools at least, had formed itself around notions of what one could say *about* language and language use. This position already looks dated. Knowing about language is one thing; but using it, making it and critiquing it are likely to be more essential features of the use of language in the first years of the present century. As communication becomes more ubiquitous and more frequent, and as a result communication management becomes more and more an essential ingredient of practice at home and at work, the emphasis on creative and critical literacy increases. No longer is it possible to be a passive user of the language without immersing oneself in consumerism and thus being prey to the whims of corporate hegemony. The active user of language, however, helps to fashion the worlds in which he/she operates. Critical literacy, it seems to me, helped us to see that reading against the text – or at least, being resistant to the ideologies that often worked surreptitiously within texts – was a first and necessary step to becoming an informed and intelligent reader and citizen. The next step is to become a more creative maker of language and manager of communication. What research has shown is that a learner who is in passive mode is less likely to develop as a language user than someone who is prepared to fashion it for him- or herself.

Another major point to emerge from the study of the nature and function of English is that the term 'English', as used to describe a loosely defined subject and discipline in schools and universities, is rapidly becoming inappropriate. 'English' may denote the language used (as opposed to French or Hindi) but it cannot for much longer be used to denote the wider programme of study that includes literatures from different countries and cultures; moving image studies; visual literacies; translations from one language to another; and studies in semiotics. The more accurate technical term is rhetoric, in the most positive sense of that word. If we take rhetoric to be the 'arts of discourse', we have a sufficiently broad but equally rigorous definition and practice within which to work. One of the many advantages of such a formulation is that it is language independent. That is to say, rhetoric can operate in whichever context it finds itself in and with whatever languages (verbal, mathematical, musical) it encounters. It removes the cultural association of 'English' with England and 'Englishness'. Pragmatically, however, it may be best to continue with the present term, however imperfect and inappropriate it is.

Extract 1.2

The young enter our classrooms full of their stories and electronic fascinations. We do them no favour if they leave with these tales and interests validated and with only the same language structures and uses they brought with them. Literary forms, ranging from fiction and drama to position papers and science reports, need introduction and mediation by experts in classrooms who know enough about everyday worlds *and* those unlikely to be in the daily world of young people to integrate the two. Teachers with such expertise know the vital need of all learners for a deep and expansive repertoire of linguistic competence. We can encourage the young to be critically reflective, politically aware and socially astute. Yet if they have not read and heard, as well as practised in meaningful roles with supportive models, the kinds of language they will need to deliberate and contest existing injustices and necessary reforms, they will remain subject to social, economic and political exploitation. Personal narratives and youth theatre telling stories of teen angst, family tensions and strains in peer relationships cannot build concepts of the hypothetical in the abstractions of the aesthetic, scientific, political or economic. We cannot depend primarily on learner interest or agency to engage the young with strong models and intensive practice. To add breadth and depth to the linguistic repertoires of the young, teachers need to imagine and enable more and more valid roles through which young people gain meaningful practice with styles, genres and types of language.

Community learning environments offer several examples of engaging roles for young learners that go beyond their immediate interests. As Miller points out in her response to Section 3, some youth groups operating almost entirely beyond the classroom take up political issues in comparative and persuasive terms. As social entrepreneurship opportunities multiply at the behest and ingenuity of the young in communities across the post-industrial world, young people set out goals and take on roles that make pertinent the need to produce and understand wide-ranging written and spoken texts (see Heath & Robinson, 2004 and Heath, 2002). Cosmopolitan culture, economic migration and the global marketplace will surely encourage more young people to see the need to go beyond the comfortable language practices of their local communities. Yet they must have guides and mediators. Why not English teachers, who will have to revisit and revalue rhetoric and know much more of structures and uses of language that cut across contexts, uses, genres and professional identities? Just as Section 2 maintains, literatures need to keep a firm place. Yet comparative literature, as well as the literature of children and young adults, should enter the hallowed domain of English literature written for adult readers.

Those of us who care about English have to disturb many common-sense truths that have entered the realm of contemporary folklore. I argue that we can do so by valuing empirical evidence on the critical need the young have for a deep and wide linguistic repertoire. Young learners in English classrooms are not mere students taking our courses but the future citizens upon whom the political and economic realities of democracies depend. We have to be strategic about expanding the funds of knowledge in which the young can and will invest if we are to ensure that their future civic participation will pay off.

Heath, S. B. (2002) Working with community, in Dees, G., Emerson, J., and Economy, P. (eds) *Strategic Tolls for Social Entrepreneurs*. New York: John Wiley.
Heath, S. B. and Robinson, K. (2004) Making a way, in Rabkin, N. and Redmond, R. (eds) *Putting the Arts in the Picture*. Chicago, IL: Columbia College.

Extract 1.3

The core issue to emerge is that teachers need to be at the centre of their own learning if they are to change their deep-seated beliefs and habits regarding the use of technology. Otherwise, surface-level adoption occurs, by which teachers just have time to learn how to use a technology without deep consideration of how it might be used to address context-specific learning needs of students. Rather than deepening and consolidating understanding of how to use the technology for enhancing learning, teachers frequently find they have to move on to learn how to use another technology or address another priority. Hammond *et al.* (2009) have iden-tified the importance of cultivating 'an inclination' to use ICT in initial teacher education. Deep-seated beliefs continue to affect CPD throughout teachers' careers. Cogill (2008) has identified the importance of a 'learning disposition' which can overcome barriers to developing with ICT, and Hansson (2006) has highlighted that 'motivation' to want to improve professionally through ICT CPD can be cultivated by 'reflecting as a teacher' and asking, 'What is in it for me? How can I improve my teaching using technology? What are the benefits for the students?' (p. 562).
 [. . .]
Boundaries between the private and the public world dissolve in many ways as a consequence of increased flexibility and user-control over the locus of work-related and private communication. One key affordance of new technologies, for example, is that they allow users to exercise control and determine whether a 'space' for communication is private or public. Users do not just generate their own content but also generate the contexts

for their learning in and across formal and informal settings (Pachler, Daly and Turvey, 2010). 'Spaces' for social networking and online participation continually evolve in ways which classrooms have never been able to do, and are certainly controlled in ways which reflect a completely different set of power relations between participants than those found in a conventional classroom. This user-centred and agentive perspective is still a long way from the experience of most learners in schools and further and higher education settings – including those which are rich in technology. The MacArthur Report (2008) claims that 'notions of expertise and authority have been turned on their heads' (p. 2) and English departments need to capitalise far more on the informal, collaborative, peer-learning networks which their students inhabit. This would constitute a considerable shift in the ways that formal education has been organised to date.

Conclusion

Electronic mobile devices, especially mobile phones with a wide range of functions, are more and more central features of our everyday lives. Yet, they remain mostly excluded from schools. While media use in everyday life and formal education belong to separate socio-cultural practice domains, the devices and services prevalent in everyday life offer considerable potential as learning resources. This we consider to be one of the main challenges in coming years for educational institutions which have been slow, on the whole, to incorporate the divergent social and cultural realities of students' lives into learning practices.

There is rich potential for technologies to become embedded in English departments in the UK – the technological infrastructure is there in most cases, and creative curriculum possibilities have begun to re-emerge. But the counter-forces at work appear to ensure that there is ongoing tension between policy and implementation, between skills agendas and professional knowledge and understanding and between technology-driven priorities and a learning agenda.

Cogill, J. (2008) Primary Teachers, Interactive Whiteboard Practice Across One Year: Changes in Pedagogy and Influencing Factors'. Unpublished doctoral thesis, King's College, University of London.

Hammond, M., Crosson, S. and Fragkouli, E. (2009) Why do Some Student Teachers Make Good Use of ICT? in *Technology, Pedagogy and Education* 18(1).

Hansson, H. (2006) 'Teachers' professional development' in *E-Learning* 3 (4).

MacArthur Report (2008) Cambridge, MA: MIT Press.

Pachler, N., Daly, C. and Turvey, A. (2010) Teacher Professional Development Practices, in Lindberg, O. and Olofsson, A. (eds) *Online Learning Communities and Teacher Professional Development*. Hershey, PA: IGI Global.

Extract 1.4

Our research shows the subject English at an important moment of transition. It is, we have suggested, being moved from being a subject that deals with values-as-meaning into one in which meanings are becoming curricularized as knowledge. Since the late 1980s, schools have experienced a long period of transition from the former state to the latter – a change that is also documented in a succession of policy documents. Admittedly, to characterize English as the subject that is or was quintessentially about meaning is a rough and ready characterization, but here we will nevertheless push it a bit further. We might say that English is the subject that has, traditionally, focused not just on meaning but on the combination of meaning-and-values. Or to be more precise, English is the subject in which *the* issue is the manner by which the meaning of values is established. In terms of the distinction between school subjects focused on knowledge and those focused on meaning it could be held that all the policy changes since the early 1990s have attempted to move English much more in the direction of turning it into a subject dealing with knowledge rather than meaning. English, to put it in sloganistic terms, is being moved in the direction of subjects such as science.

There might be three objections to this at once. The first would be that all school subjects convey or enact values – value production is one of the central features of the work of the school. To this we would say that English differs from other subjects and practices, in that 'values' and 'meaning-making' are closely woven into its ideational work. Second, those who teach subjects such as religious education, for instance, will insist that they are and have always been interested in values. That is no doubt the case; it is our contestation that it is the conjunction of meaning and values – the question 'By what processes are the meanings of these or those values established?' – that had made English different and distinctive. The third objection is a much newer one, one which would say: 'Well, actually, English is not all that different any more; because while English is being pushed in the direction of explicitness in curriculum, subjects such as science are undergoing a move in the other direction'. As science ceases to be the subject that gives access to the discipline for the purposes of becoming a 'scientist', let's say, and is moving in the direction of providing essential information for informed participation in public life – often labelled by the inappropriate term 'scientific literacy' – it begins to deal with matters of ethics, for instance, of understanding the implications of scientific work on matters of everyday issues such as nutrition, health or the environment. There is, it seems, something like a 'crossover' in the trajectories of the two subjects.

We are, as we point out above, aware that we may be overstating the case, but it is nevertheless, we think, a discernible trend. In each case the motivation seems the same: to make the subject fit contemporary social and economic demands – the demands of competent communication in the one case, and of informed citizenship in the other. What differs in each case is the (assumed or actual) starting point in the movement of the two subjects.

To what extent this trend appears in any specific classroom varies, as we have shown; it is dependent on what social factors are in play, and in what combinations. However, what our research shows clearly is that while *direction from above* has effects to a certain extent, and maybe even in partially predictable ways, these ways are predictable not from the contents of the policies so much but rather much more from the mix of social factors to which we have drawn attention: does the school operate a policy of selection?; does it have a policy of streaming?; what kinds of departmental culture does it enable?; how does it perceive its local environment from a number of different perspectives?; and so on. These factors are of course in some senses the outcomes of national policy – a policy that favours 'diversity' between schools and selectiveness within them. In other senses, they are the product of other sorts of histories, experiences and commitments. Their effect is to ensure that English is always 'inflected': they position teachers differently in relation to their local practice in the English classroom, and supply them with different resources, perspectives and constraints. Here, at classroom level, it is the actions of the various agents in the 'mix' that are the telling factors, and the decisions that are made that have real effects on the appearance of the subject.

Extract 1.5

English is more attuned to the Enlightenment project than has usually been assumed. I have suggested that, if not in the obvious ways we readily recognise in, say, biology, its business, too, is the promotion of knowledge and, beyond that (as should be equally true of the teaching of the other academic subjects) the mind's organisation and philosophical reflection.

The general point of the argument has been to try to relocate English in terms of a reactivated general vision of education, one that will necessarily have Enlightenment values at its core. Behind this aim is the notion that to find its proper direction English needs to start from an idea of education before an idea of the subject. I think 'education' has a meaning that goes beyond the definitions of the separate subjects and that what teachers should be serving is primarily education rather than this or that subject, which they should think of as their own particular way, among others, of making education happen. Writing an exact definition of education, one capable of being 'operationalised' in research or assessment, would be as impossible as writing one for virtue; but amongst those of us who have undergone a formation, in and out of school, implicitly shaped on Enlightenment lines, there would be wide agreement in recognising it when it shows up. Knowledge and reason would be prominent, but also a proper respect for values to do with human relations: humanity, belief in the shared humanity of all men and women, regard for others and acknowledgement of intuition, feeling and imagination. Contrary to popular belief, these values, too, were central to the thinking of philosophers such as Hume, Adam Smith and Kant.

The account of the Enlightenment that should be our reference point takes as central the philosophies of David Hume and Adam Smith for whom feeling – 'moral sentiment' and 'aesthetic response' – were as important as reason and rationality; the point was to keep the two in their proper spheres and, relevantly for us, to confine rational calculation to those areas, such as manufacturing and scientific investigation, where it was appropriate. In this view (Day 1996) the radical early works of Wordsworth and Coleridge were Enlightenment products, before the poet's Romantic retreat into anti-rationalism, feeling, 'cherishing private souls' (Inglis 1973; Barnes, Barnes, and Clarke 1984) and, of course, political reaction. And Enlightenment writers include Tom Paine, Mary Wollstonecraft and William Blake: it was radicalism as well as Augustan politeness.

An insistence on English as a development of *mind* as well as *soul*, of knowledge and cognitive capability as well as emotional and aesthetic response, is necessary to counteract the anti-intellectualism that has at times dominated English (Medway 1990), ultimately deriving, according to Reid (2003) from Wordsworth's Romanticism. Perhaps more relevant at the moment is a principled philosophy with which to discredit the current

Benthamite version of rationality that governs the management of the entire public sector in England, prizing rational *means* – efficient mechanisms of 'delivery' – and dismissing humane *ends* as impractically nebulous. Bentham's and Gradgrind's utilitarianism (one of Gradgrind's children was named Malthus!) was a bastard child of the Enlightenment, stripped of the humanity that characterised at least the eighteenth century Scottish philosophers (Whale 2000). In education this has meant a rationalist reduction of learning to interchangeable modules, defined stages and targets, so that studying Sylvia Plath can be assessed and accredited as commensurable with learning some procedure in Hospitality and Tourism. (What's in play is a *rhetoric* of rationality rather than the principled real thing; the practice is often far from rational, for instance in its frequent casual disregard for evidence.)

A view of education as still essentially an Enlightenment undertaking would give us a basis on which to reconstruct our institutions, and English teachers need have no hesitation in claiming a central place in it providing they direct their particular practice by the same lights.

Barnes, D., Barnes, D. and Clarke, S. (1984) *Versions of English*. London: Heinemann.

Day, A. (1996) *Romanticism*. London: Routledge.

Inglis, B. (1973) Against proportional representation, in *English in Education* 9(1).

Medway, P. (1990) Into the sixties, in Goodson, I. and Medway, P. (eds) *Bringing English to Order*. London: Falmer.

Reid, I. (2004) *Wordsworth and the Formation of English Studies*. Aldershot: Ashgate Publishing.

Whale, J. (2000) *Imagination Under Pressure 1789–1832*. Cambridge: Cambridge University Press.

Exploratory questions

- Following Andrews' summary, does recent research suggest ways forward? What do you consider to be both the opportunities and the threats in the future of school-based English?

- Brice Heath talks of the need to 'disturb many common-sense truths' about English in the curriculum and beyond; do you share this view? Which myths in particular would you wish to dispel?

- Following Daly's exposition, how important do you consider ICT in the development of English? Are the differences technologies introduce likely to be profound or merely superficial?

- Kress and colleagues state that 'English is the subject in which *the* issue is the manner by which the meaning of values is established', and view the possibilities of the future accordingly; do you agree, essentially?
- I have responded to Medway's paper (Stevens, D. (2011) Critically Enlightened Romantic Values and English Pedagogy: A Response to Peter Medway, in *Changing English* 18.1, 45–56) in defence of Romanticism as a basis of English; what do you make of his insistence on Enlightenment values? How does his view relate to your own personal and professional sense of the subject English?
- From your own reading, including authors represented in this book, and professional experience, what trends do you discern in the development of English pedagogy? Where, if anywhere, may you, and your colleagues, make a tangible difference?

Further reading

Many of the books and papers either excerpted from or recommended for further reading throughout the present anthology in the contexts of particular thematic chapters offer visions of the future of English pedagogy – either utopian, dystopian or (more usually) somewhere between. For this reason, there is no specific further reading on future possibilities. Indeed, I urge all practitioners – practising and student teachers – to forge a cohesive, creative and critically aware future for the subject English, making positive use of the thoughts presented here (alongside many others) as touchstones.

Index for *A Guided Reader for Secondary English.*